INVOLVEMENT OF CHILDREN A

Studia Paedagogica

INVOLVEMENT OF CHILDREN AND TEACHER STYLE

INSIGHTS FROM AN INTERNATIONAL STUDY ON EXPERIENTIAL EDUCATION

Edited by Ferre LAEVERS and Ludo HEYLEN

Leuven University Press
2003

SOCRATES programme Action 6.1.2
"General activities of observation and innovation"

With the support of
K.U.Leuven Commissie voor Publicaties

ISBN 90 5867 342 1

D / 2003 / 1869 / 68

NUR: 847

CONTENT

INTRODUCTION

The innovative project "Experiential Education" (EXE) originated in 1976 from a close collaboration between a research unit at the Department of Educational Sciences (University of Leuven) and practitioners in the area of early childhood and primary education. Both at the conceptual and at the level of practice this project generated a framework for quality assessment and quality improvement relevant for any context aiming at the development of persons, from toddlers to in-service training.

The project, still in progress, is regarded in Flanders and in the Netherlands as one of the most influential innovative movements of the nineties in the field of early childhood and primary education. But since 1991 the story of Experiential Education has an international dimension. Thanks to a series of European Comenius projects Experiential Education became more and more a product of international collaboration and an example of the impact of impulses by the European Commission.
The result of the Socrates project reported in this volume builds on the networks formed during the past decade.

Conceptual basis

The partners gathered in this project found a common base for their activities in the 'process-oriented approach' that belongs to the core of Experiential Education. The key-elements of this framework are: (i) well-being and involvement as indicators for quality; (ii) insights about ways to enhance well-being and involvement in children and adults; (iii) a theoretical basis for the description and assessment of outcomes, captured by the concept of deep-level learning.

The experiential approach focuses on the well-being and the involvement. These variables refer to the process in the learner. They describe qualities that can be observed in the child or adult while the 'teaching' is taking place; that is why they can be categorised as 'process variables'. Well-being and involvement are generated by an educational context or learning environment and give direct feedback about the impact of the interventions of the teacher (context variables). They also are linked to the outcomes: well-being and involvement are the indirect but at least actual and tangible indicators for the quality of the learning process. They give a fair idea about the chances for a positive personal, social-emotional and cognitive development of the learner.

Objectives

The aim of the project is to explore in depth how the process-oriented approach can improve the quality of education and teaching in a wide variety of contexts, that is: (i) in several European countries with different traditions and cultures, (ii) in settings going from early childhood education up to the field of the professional development of teachers and (iii) in institutions with differing profiles, ranging from research centres to teacher training institutes.

Methodology

On top of the wide range of contexts comes the great variation in position of the partners as to their acquaintance with the process-oriented approach. Some institutions have been using concepts of Experiential Education since the beginning of the nineties. Others were starting to assimilate the concepts when they joined this Socrates project. This heterogeneous condition demanded an appropriate strategy giving room for a multitude of actions but offering at the same time a common platform for exchange and collaboration. To achieve this two EXE-instruments were defined as the common denominator of our joined actions: the Leuven Involvement Scale and the Adult Style Observation Schedule (ASOS). Each of the partners committed themselves to take initiatives in which either or both of these concepts and instruments are used.

A shared framework in a variety of contexts

Throughout the contributions a series of themes can be identified documenting the diversity of questions and methods and at the same time showing the framework that has been shared by all the partners.
In relation with involvement and the related scale, Michaela Ulich and Tony Mayr undertake an in depth analysis of the concept of involvement, explore the process of adoption of the scale by practitioners in the context of German early childhood settings and reflect on the relations between levels of involvement and child characteristics. In this, patterns linked to gender, to ethnic origin and to age level are explored.

Maria Nabuco and Silvério Prates worked with pre-primary teachers in Portugal. Using a pre- and post-test design she registers – with the Early Childhood Environment Rating Scale-Revised (ECERS-R) - the evolution in the quality of teaching and confronts these measures with the observed levels of involvement of children.

8

In Diane Doble Leemans' study we get a closer look into the interaction between adult and child (in a pre-primary setting and in the context of art education). The meticulous analysis of video-recordings reveals how teacher style in a subtle way determines involvement and affects the process of 'construction of meaning' that is at the heart of expression.

The contribution of Christine Pascal and Tony Bertram is dedicated to the Adult Style Observation Schedule (ASOS) and covers a large amount of empirical data in a variety of settings in the U.K.. They explore (i) what kind of patterns in adult style are displayed when comparing practitioners in a variety of early childhood education and care settings and (ii) how in-service training can improve the quality of the adult child interactions.

Marjatta Kalliala and Leena Tahkokallio combine both quality indicators in their study: with the Involvement Scale and the ASOS they gather systematically data in Finnish childcare settings. Their research design allows to gain insight into the impact of in-service training on adult style, to learn more about the process that leads to an effective style and to compare the assessed patterns with research data from practitioners in the U.K.

Julia Formosinho addresses the two variables – involvement and teacher style – but separately. For the first a qualitative analysis of early years teachers' thoughts about the use of the Involvement Scale proves to be an interesting approach to understanding how taking on board the concept of involvement gradually informs practice. For adult style we get, again, a comparative analysis of patterns recorded in Portuguese and in English pre-primary teachers and caretakers.

With the contribution of Gabriela Portugal and Paulo Santos we stay in Portugal but shift from the education and care sector to the professional support of families living in difficult conditions. They adapt the Adult Style Observation Schedule to serve as a guide for social workers operating in this particular field of action. This exercise offers insights about the conceptual basis of the ASOS and reveals at the same time how the three dimensions – Stimulation – Sensitivity – Autonomy - can help to monitor the interventions of support workers.

Peter Van Sanden and An Joly's contribution brings us to a different context – early childhood and primary education in Nicaragua -, but again testifies how the concept of involvement can be inspirational in improving the quality of teaching. The reconstruction of the process of adoption of involvement as an indicator of quality, helps us to identify a general pattern in the way teachers develop a process-oriented approach, that is, learn to take the perspective of the child.

Finally, the chapter written by Ludo Heylen shifts from early years practice to teacher training. Here involvement is at the centre of a self-assessment instrument enabling students to report their degree of involvement (and well-being) in each of the parts of the curriculum. Brought together, these data are a rich source for further analysis by the staff. But in a direct way, learning to assess ones own level of involvement prepares the students to take that perspective with them as teachers.

Time table

The project started in January 2001 and was concluded in January 2002. Only two meetings were organised. A workshop in May brought the partners together (i) to share their insights concerning the key concepts involvement and style, (ii) to inform one another about the initiatives taken and the provisory results and (iii) to prepare the second meeting planned for December 2001. The latter was an open International Conference, held in Leuven in which each of the partners presented the results of their work.

Evaluation

When looking at the harvest of this Socrates project – reported in the chapters of this book - one can only be impressed by the many insights that were generated through the network of partners. It is obvious that the chosen strategy – focusing on two central concepts – proved to be effective and the right way to deal with the enormous range of contexts and methodologies used by the several partners. But this publication reflects only one part of the added value of the exchange. Another part should be mentioned: the atmosphere, the intense mental activity and the sharing of sometimes fascinating, sometimes challenging ideas. Throughout the richness brought by the variety in backgrounds, cultures and contexts it was obvious that certain values, at a more profound level, served as a common ground and facilitated communication and mutual respect. This is the way a European identity is shaped while diversity still functions as an endless source for new questions and exploration. The project is closed. The process is still going on.

Acknowledgement

It is with pleasure and sincerity that we express our gratitude to all who have contributed to the publication of this volume. To begin with the European Commission and the financial support within the Socrates program that allowed us to organise our meetings and the international Conference that was at the centre of our strategy. I thank all the authors for fulfilling their engagement to bring their part of the project to an end and for the intense collaboration that made this project succeed. We are very grateful for the financial support of the Leuven University Press and the Department of Educational Sciences who agreed to invest in the publication of this volume in the series Studia Paedagogica. Finally our special thanks go to Bart Declercq who was a great support in finalizing the draft version of this publication.

Leuven
November 2003
F.L. & L.H.

EXPERIENTIAL EDUCATION:
MAKING CARE AND EDUCATION MORE EFFECTIVE
THROUGH WELL-BEING AND INVOLVEMENT

Ferre Laevers

In May 1976 twelve Flemish pre-school teachers, assisted by two educational consultants, start a series of sessions with the intention to reflect critically upon their practice. Their approach is 'experiential': the intention is to make a close, moment by moment description of what it means to a young child to live and take part in the educational setting. This careful observation and 'reconstruction' of the child's experiences brings to light a series of unsatisfactory conditions. Too many opportunities to sustain children's development remain unused. During the following tens of sessions the group discusses possible solutions for the problems they meet, work them out in practice and reflect on their experiences. Gradually they begin to realise how much they have moved away from current pre-school practice. A new educational model for pre-school is taking shape: Experiential Education (EXE). It grew further to become one of the most influential educational models in the area of elementary education in Flanders and the Netherlands. From 1991 the dissemination in other European countries, including the UK, took off.

EXE offers a conceptual basis that proved to be useful in other contexts such as child care, special education, secondary education, teacher training and any kind of setting where learning and professional development is meant to take place.

1 In search of quality

What constitutes 'quality' in care and education? From the point of view of the parent, the counsellor, the head teacher, the curriculum developer the question is very often answered by expressing expectations with regard to the educational context and the teacher's actions: the infrastructure and equipment, the content of activities, teaching methods, teacher style... From the point of view of policy and government there is a more direct reference to the expected outcomes of education. With regular assessments the system of care and education, in a sense, is 'forced' to get better results. In the middle of this stands the practitioner, living and working with children. Wanting the best for them. Accepting sensible guidelines and accepting at the same time the fact that education has to be effective. But how to combine all those things and get the two ends - context and outcome - together?

2 Focusing on the process

The project Experiential Education's most important contribution answers exactly this question, by identifying indicators for quality that are situated just in the middle of the two approaches. It points to the missing link: the concept that helps us to sense if what we are doing (the context) is leading to somewhere (the outcome)!

Figure 1: Context – Process-Outcomes Scheme

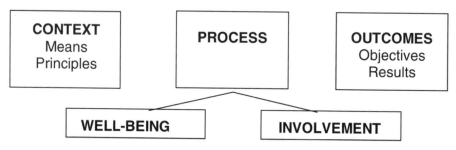

The basic insight within the EXE-theory is that the most economic and conclusive way to assess the quality of any educational setting (from the pre-school level to adult education) is to focus on two dimensions: the degree of 'emotional well-being' and the level of 'involvement'.

When we want to know how each of the children is doing in a setting, we first have to explore the degree in which children do feel at ease, act spontaneously, show vitality and self-confidence. All this indicates that their emotional well-being is ok and that their physical needs, the need for tenderness and affection, the need for safety and clarity, the need for social recognition, the need to feel competent and the need for meaning in life and moral value are satisfied.

The second criterion is linked to the developmental process and urges the adult to set up a challenging environment favouring involvement.

Good schools have to succeed on both tasks: only paying attention to emotional well-being and a positive climate is not enough, while efforts to enhance involvement will only have an impact if children and students feel at home and are free from emotional constraints.

14

3 Involvement, the key word

The concept of involvement refers to a dimension of human activity. Involvement is not linked to specific types of behaviour nor to specific levels of development. Both the baby in the cradle playing with his voice and the adult trying to formulate a definition, both the (mentally) handicapped child and the gifted student, can share that quality. Csikszentmihayli (1979) speaks of "the state of flow".

One of the most predominant characteristics of this flow state is concentration. An involved person is narrowing his attention to one limited circle. Involvement goes along with strong motivation, fascination and total implication: there is no distance between person and activity, no calculation of the possible benefits. Because of that, time perception is distorted (time passes by rapidly). Furthermore there is an openness to (relevant) stimuli and the perceptual and cognitive functioning has an intensity, lacking in activities of another kind. The meanings of words and ideas are felt more strongly and deeply. Further analysis reveals a manifest feeling of satisfaction and a bodily felt stream of positive energy. The 'state of flow' is sought actively by people. Young children find it most of the time in play.

Of course, one could describe a variety of situations where we can speak of satisfaction combined with intense experience, but not all of them would match our concept of involvement. Involvement is not the state of arousal easily obtained by the entertainer. The crucial point is that the satisfaction stems from one source: the exploratory drive, the need to get a better grip on reality, the intrinsic interest in how things and people are, the urge to experience and figure out. Only when we succeed in activating the exploratory drive do we get the intrinsic type of involvement and not just involvement of an emotional or functional kind.

Finally, involvement only occurs in the small area in which the activity matches the capabilities of the person, that is in the 'zone of proximal development'.

To conclude: involvement means that there is intense mental activity, that a person is functioning at the very limits of his or her capabilities, with an energy flow that comes from intrinsic sources. One couldn't think of any condition more favourable to real development. If we want deep-level-learning, we cannot do without involvement.

4 Measuring involvement

However much involvement may seem to be a subjective property, it is very well possible to assess in a reliable way the levels of involvement in children and adults. For this the "Leuven Involvement Scale" (LIS) has been developed, encompassing seven variants for different settings, ranging from childcare to adult education.

The LIS is a 5-point rating scale. At level 1, there is no activity. The child is mentally absent. If we can see some action it is a purely stereotypic repetition of very elementary movements. Level 2 doesn't go further than actions with many interruptions. At level 3, we can without a doubt label the child's behaviour as an activity. The child is doing something (e.g. listening to a story, making something with clay, experimenting in the sand table, interacting with others, writing, reading, finishing a task...). But we miss concentration, motivation and pleasure in the activity. In many cases the child is functioning at a routine level. In level 4 moments of intense mental activity occur. At level 5 there is total involvement expressed by concentration and absolute implication. Any disturbance or interruption would be experienced as a frustrating rupture of a smoothly running activity.

The core of the rating process consists of an act of empathy in which the observer has to get into the experience of the child, in a sense has to become the child. This gives the information to draw conclusions concerning the mental activity of the child and the intensity of his experience. Despite of the required observational skills, the inter-scorer reliability of the LIS-YC (a comparison between two observers) is .90 and thus very satisfactory.

Research with the Leuven Involvement Scale has shown that the levels of involvement within a setting tend to be more or less stable (Laevers, 1994). They are the result of the interactions between the context (including the way teachers handle their group) and the characteristics of the children. We can expect that the more competent the teacher, the higher the level of involvement can be, given a particularly composed group of children. We find indications for this in our own research, but also in the large scale Effective Early Learning project in the UK, where more than 3.000 adults learned to use the scale and more than 30.000 children at the pre-school age have been observed with it (Pascal & Bertram, 1995; Pascal et al., 1998).

5 Raising the levels of well-being and involvement

The concepts of well-being and involvement are not only useful for research purposes, but at least as much for practitioners who want to improve the quality of their work. Capitalising on a myriad of experiences by teachers, a body of expertise has been gathered and systematised in The Ten Action Points, an inventory of ten types of initiatives that favour well-being and involvement (Laevers & Moons, 1997).

THE TEN ACTION POINTS

1. Rearrange the classroom in appealing corners or areas
2. Check the content of the corners and replace unattractive materials by more appealing ones
3. Introduce new and unconventional materials and activities
4. Observe children, discover their interests and find activities that meet these orientations
5. Support ongoing activities through stimulating impulses and enriching interventions
6. Widen the possibilities for free initiative and support them with sound rules and agreements
7. Explore the relation with each of the children and between children and try to improve it
8. Introduce activities that help children to explore the world of behaviour, feelings and values
9. Identify children with emotional problems and work out sustaining interventions
10. Identify children with developmental needs and work out interventions that engender involvement within the problem area

---

The action points cover a wide range of interventions. In AP1, 2 and 3 the organization of the space and the provision of interesting materials and activities is at stake. With AP4, the teacher is invited to observe carefully how children interact with all that they encounter in their environment in order to identify interests that can be met by a more targeted offer of activities. It is on this track that open projects come to life. They gradually take shape building upon what children indicate as points of interest in their responses to a former offer. The realisation of a rich environment doesn't stop with the provision of a wide variety of potentially interesting materials and activities. A decisive element in the occurrence of involvement is the way the adult supports the ongoing activities with stimulating interventions (AP5) which are part of an effective adult style.

Using the dynamics in children and their exploratory drive requires an open form of organisation that stimulates children to take initiative (AP6). That is why in EXE-settings, children are free to choose between a wide range of activities (up to about 65 % of the available time). This point includes the setting of rules that guarantee a smoothly running class organisation and a maximum of freedom for every child (and not only for the fittest and the most assertive ones). It takes months to get this far with a group of children. But the efforts to implement this open form are rewarded. Research indicates that - given a rich offer - the more children can choose their activities, the higher the levels of involvement.

In AP7 the field of social relations is addressed. The adult not only explores the relations between the children, but also tries to be aware of how she/he is experienced by children. Guidelines in this area encompass qualities already defined by Carl Rogers (empathy and authenticity). At the group level explicit attention is given to the creation of opportunities to share experiences and build a positive group climate.

In AP8 activities are generated that support the exploration of feelings, thoughts and values. In a sense it is a promotion of psychology as a field of competence, but of course at the level of young children. One of the materials supporting the development of social cognition, is the Box Full of Feelings. The series of open ended activities linked to the set, helps children to develop emotional intelligence and social competence. The effect has been reported by Nanette Smith, finishing a dissertation on this subject, on a BBC programme for practitioners: "We've only used the Box Full of Feelings for seven weeks. Already we've seen a big, significant difference. (-) we can sense a general feeling of protectiveness, awareness, friendship and empathy in the children which wasn't there before. (Kog, Moons & Depondt, 1997)."

6 Children who need special attention

AP1 to 8 have a general character: they lay the foundations. The two remaining action points turn our attention to children needing special attention because they do not reach the levels of well-being and involvement that we strive for. In the first (AP9) we deal with behavioural and emotional problems: children who, through all kinds of circumstances, do not succeed in realising a satisfying interaction with their environment, who come under pressure and lose contact with their inner stream of experiences. On the basis of a large number of case-studies, an experiential strategy has been developed to help them. Interventions

18

that proved effective range from "giving positive attention and support" to "giving security by structuring time and space".

The last action point (AP10) is about children with special developmental needs. We define them as children that fail to come to activity in which the quality of 'involvement' is realised in one or more areas of competence. This means that their development is endangered and chances are real that they will not develop the potential they have in them.

Teacher interventions can vary a lot, depending on the nature of activities or on the responses and initiatives of children. Nevertheless, we can discern individual patterns in the way one intervenes in a wide variety of situations. The notion of 'style' is used to grasp this pattern.

The 'Adult Style Observation Schedule' (ASOS) is built around three dimensions: stimulation, sensitivity and giving autonomy (Laevers, Bogaerts & Moons, 1997).

Stimulating interventions are open impulses that engender a chain of actions in children and make the difference between low and high involvement. Such as: suggesting activities to children that wander around, offering materials that fit in an ongoing activity, inviting children to communicate, confronting them with thought-provoking questions and giving them information that can capture their mind.

Sensitivity is evidenced in responses that witness empathic understanding of the basic needs of the child, such as, the need for security, for affection, for attention, for affirmation, for clarity and for emotional support.

Giving autonomy in not only realised in the open form of organisation but has to be implemented as well at the level of interventions. It means: to respect children's sense for initiative by acknowledging their interests, giving them room for experimentation, letting them decide upon the way an activity is performed and when a product is finished, implicate them in the setting of rules and the solution of conflicts.

Once we begin to look at the way adults interact with children we realise how powerful these dimensions are. In view of getting high levels of well-being and involvement the person of the teacher is even more important than other dimensions of the context, such as the space, the material and the activities on offer.

19

7 The Process-Oriented Child Monitoring System

To identify children who need special attention systematic observation is necessary and, in fact, one or another kind of monitoring system. Although the traditional product-oriented systems have their value, especially for diagnostic purposes, they also have serious limitations. The first is that using them at a group level leads to an enormous investment, leaving no time for real interventions. Further, most systems concentrate on typical academic achievements and do forget that success is often more dependent on learning dispositions. Finally, having discovered where a child stands does not mean one knows immediately which actions to take. The paradigm behind most monitoring systems seems to be that one just has to break down the task further to help the child overcome the gap. But this approach doesn't take the nature of developmental processes into account and that the child functions as a whole.

Totally in consistence with the EXE-framework, the Process-oriented Monitoring System (the POMS) focuses onto the two major indications for the quality of the educational process: well-being and involvement. These give the answer to the essential question: how is each child doing? Are the efforts we make sufficient to secure emotional health and real development in all important areas and for each of the children? In a first step, children are screened, with a five point scale for each of the dimensions. For children falling below level 4, teachers proceed with further observations and analysis. A periodic assessment (3 or 4 times a year) of these levels has shown to be practicable and effective. In contrast to other systems, the POMS gives a sense of purpose: teachers get immediate feedback about the quality of their work and can get to work without delay. The target being to evoke enjoyment and more intrinsic motivated action within the fields of development that are at stake (Laevers, 1997).

8 Deep-level-learning

In the EXE-theoretical framework, a lot of attention is paid to the effects or outcomes of education. The concept of 'deep-level-learning', expresses the concern for a critical approach of educational evaluation. Central to this is the questioning of superficial learning, learning that does not affect the basic competencies of the child and has little transfer to real life situations. In line with a constructivist tradition, we don't see the process of development as a mere addition of discrete elements of knowledge or aptitudes to an existing repertoire. On the contrary: every performance is depending on an underlying structure of fundamental schemes. These operate as basic programmes that regulate the way we process incoming stimuli and construct reality. By them we interpret new situations and we act competently - or not. They determine which and how many dimensions of reality can be articulated in ones perception and cognition (Laevers, 1995 & 1998).

The ongoing research programme in which instruments are developed to assess levels of development, covers five areas of development: (1) physical knowledge; (2) psycho-social cognition; (3) communication and expression; (4) creativity and (5) self-organisation.

In this context the exploration of forms of intelligence based on intuitive faculties, as opposed to the logical-mathematical intelligence, gets special attention. Real understanding of the world is built on the capacity to get the feel of it. Consequently, the difference in competence between people, in any profession that requires a certain level of understanding, is made by their intuitive view on the matter. This is the case for physicists, medical doctors, biologists, geologists, engineers... but also in any craft where routine and technique is to be transcended and interpretations have to be made. This also holds for the field of psycho-social cognition. Intuition is the core of the expertise in professions where dealing with people plays an important role, such as, child care, teaching, all kinds of therapies, human resources management, advertising and of course in all the sciences connected to these. This domain is one of the most fascinating ones and can be seen as one of the challenges for educational research in the next century.

9 Value education

Within the EXE-project the concept of 'linkedness' is the expression of the deep concern for the development of a positive orientation towards reality. It offers a point of reference for the whole of value education.

Linkedness with the eco-system in its entirety is essentially a religious concept, in the broadest sense of the word. Etymologically, 're-ligion' (re-liare) means 'linking again'. As "de-linquency" means "the lack of being linked", the sense of 'connectedness' can be seen as the cornerstone of prevention of criminal behaviour or any action that brings damage to things and people. One who feels connected with something would not act as a vandal.

In the elaboration of the concept at the level of pre-school education, children are helped to develop this attitude of linkedness with (1) themselves, (2) the other(s), (3) the material world, (4) society and (5) the ultimate unity of the entire eco-system.

10 It is about energy

Experiences accumulated in the EXE project support the conclusion that well-being and involvement, are welcomed by teachers as most stimulating and helpful to improve the quality of their work. The concepts of well-being and involvement match the intuitions of many teachers and give them a scientifically-based confirmation of what they knew already: when we can get children in that 'flow state', development must and will take place within the area(s) addressed by the activity. In contrast to effect variables – the real outcomes are only seen on the longer run – the process variables give immediate feedback about the quality of (planned) interventions and tell us on the spot something about the potential impact. Furthermore, putting forward involvement as key indicator for quality, engenders a lot of positive energy and synergy: the enthusiastic responses of children, when teaching efforts are successful, are very empowering and give the teacher deep satisfaction both at the professional and personal level. Finally, taking involvement as a point of reference in the guidance of professionals makes it possible to respect the actual level of functioning of the teacher and the setting. For the implementation of experiential education, one starts where one stands, with the room, the children, the material, the books, the methods and all the limitations linked to the actual situation. Then a field of action is chosen and initiatives are taken that have the potential to bring about an increase in well-being and/or involvement. This increase – even how small it may be - is experienced as a success and drives one towards new initiatives.

That is what Experiential Education is about: exploiting and enhancing the energy in people and bringing them into a positive spiral that engenders deep-level-learning in the child... and in the adult!

References

Csikszentmihayli, M. (1979). The concept of flow. In B. Sutton-Smith, *Play and learning* (pp. 257-273). New York: Gardner.

Laevers, F. (1993). Deep-level-learning: An exemplary application on the area of physical knowledge. *European Early Childhood Research Journal, 1*, 53 - 68.

Laevers, F. (Ed.) (1994). *Defining and assessing quality in early childhood education.* Leuven: Leuven University Press.

Laevers, F. (1994). The innovative project "Experiential Education" and the definition of quality in education. In F. Laevers (Ed.), *Defining and assessing quality in early childhood education* (pp. 159-172). Leuven: Leuven University Press.

Laevers, F. (Ed.) (1994). *The Leuven Involvement Scale for Young Children* [manual and videotape]. Leuven: Centre for Experiential Education.

Laevers, F. (1994). Early childhood education in Flanders, Belgium. In H. Vejleskov (1994), *Early childhood care and education: 11 countries* (pp. 21-34). Dundee: CIDREE.

Laevers, F. (1997). Assessing the quality of childcare provision: "Involvement" as criterion. *Researching Early Childhood, 3*, 151-165.

Laevers, F. (1998). Understanding the world of objects and of people: Intuition as the core element of deep-level-learning. *International Journal of Educational Research, 29*, 69-85.

Pascal, E. & Bertram, T. (1995). "Involvement" and the Effective Early Learning Project: A collaborative venture. In F. Laevers (Ed.), *An exploration of the concept of "involvement" as an indicator of the quality of early childhood care and education* [CIDREE Report, Volume 10] (pp. 25 – 38). Dundee: CIDREE.

Pascal, E. et al. (1998). Exploring the relationship between process and outcome in young children's learning: stage one of a longitudinal study. *International Journal of Educational Research, 29*, 51-67.

Practice oriented publications from the Centre for Experiential Education

Laevers, F. & Moons, J.(1997). *Enhancing well-being and involvement in children. An introduction in the ten action points* [videotape]. Leuven: Centre for Experiential Education.
[A video based on more than 100 slides with English spoken comment.]

Laevers, F., Bogaerts M. & Moons, J. (1997). *Experiential Education at Work. A setting with 5-year olds* [manual and videotape]. Leuven: Centre for Experiential Education.
[A video-impression with a guide to analyse the sequences from the point of view of adult style, the ten action points and the developmental domains.]

Kog, M., Moons, J. & Depondt, L. (1997). *A Box full of feelings* [a playset for children from 3 to 8]. Leuven: Centre for Experiential Education.
[A case with 4 posters, 4 little cases, 48 situational pictures, finger puppets, a set of worksheets to be copied and a manual describing more than 20 different activities]

Laevers, F., Vandenbussche E., Kog, M., & Depondt, L. (1997). *A process-oriented child monitoring system for young children*. Leuven: Centre for Experiential Education.
[A manual covering 3 stages, from group screening to interventions, with 8 forms to support all the process and ideas for interventions]

Implementing the Involvement Scales in German day care centres: Practitioners perspectives, theoretical issues, empirical findings

Michaela Ulich, Toni Mayr

With increasing international co-operation, pedagogic concepts, observation methods and instruments that were developed in one specific educational culture and context (e.g. ECERS or the Child Behaviour Checklist in the US) come to be used in different countries. In our project a child observation scheme from Flanders was implemented in Southern Germany. This type of migration should always be accompanied by a careful scrutiny of the educational culture of the receiving country, as it may, on a very practical level, affect practitioners' readiness and competence in using the methods that have been imported. Likewise, such a process of international exchange also means that a specific theory (in this case the concept of involvement) must be seen in the context of theoretical discussions and empirical work in the international scientific community.

Our findings and conclusions concerning the implementation of the involvement concept and scales in Germany are based (a) on a 2-year research project with practitioners implementing the involvement scales, (b) semi-structured interviews on child observation with practitioners (c) in-service training of practitioners and professionals in teacher training institutions and (d) the presentations at German conferences on early childhood education and development. Our discussion will address 3 different levels of implementation:

- Practitioners' attitudes and practices concerning child observation and assessment
- Theoretical-methodological questions around the concept of involvement and its observation
- The Involvement Activities Scale as an instrument for centre-based quality development

1 Practitioners attitudes and practices concerning child observation and assessment

How does an observation scheme that was developed in a specific setting (Flanders) fit into a different early childhood setting (Germany) and its culture of child observation? How did the practitioners in Germany, in our sample (N=67), relate to this specific method of child observation and assessment (cf. Ulich & Mayr, 1999ab)?

To begin with we studied practitioners' attitudes towards systematic child observation – both prior to the project and during implementation. When German practitioners are asked about their observation practice they will - as a rule - reply that observing children is very important for their work, that they do it most of the time as a matter of course (naturally). In this case they are referring to "spontaneous observation" and this type of observation was not what we were interested in. Thus, at the onset of our interviews, we made the distinction between "planned" and "spontaneous" observation and pointed out that all ensuing questions would refer to planned and focused observations. The interview was structured around the following leading questions:

- what methods of child observation are you familiar with?
- what did you learn about child observation methods in your initial and in-service training?
- what type of observation do you practise, who and what is observed on what occasion?
- how do you take notes or document your observations, when do you use them?
- what keeps you from observing children in your daily practice?

1.1 Attitudes toward systematic child observation

The most significant overall finding is the low priority that is attributed to systematic child observation – both in training and practice (cf. Mayr & Ulich, 1998; Ulich & Mayr 1999a). This low priority is clearly related to some implicit and explicit traditions and ideologies in German kindergarten culture. We will only mention a few (cf. Ulich & Mayr, 1999a).

1.1.1 THE HOLISTIC MYTH

The method that is most familiar to practitioners is the unstructured observation of the whole child. Kindergarten training and ideology seem to socialise practitioners into a predominantly holistic view of the child – which implies that we should always see the child as whole, that the play and learning experiences of the young child involve the child as whole. This is a very important idea and we do not want to question this ideal as a basic principle in early childhood education and development. The holistic view becomes a

26

problem when this ideal builds up a sort of psychological barrier making practitioners very defensive about observing and analysing specific areas or aspects of child behaviour; they feel they are not doing justice to the "whole child".

1.1.2 ASSESSING CHILDREN MEANS GRADING AND LABELLING CHILDREN

Assessing children's behaviour with a structured scheme and a scale ranging from 1 to 5 is associated with giving marks, with pinpointing and labelling children. For one, this fear is associated with the holistic ideal; at the same time it is also related to a larger context: namely the traditional separation and even polarisation between kindergarten and school. Some markers across the dividing line are:

- "in kindergarten children do not get marks for what they do"
- "kindergarten it is not an achievement oriented or competitive system"
- "in kindergarten children should have the chance to develop at their own pace"

This ideal may be endangered by a uniform, structured system of observation, a systematic comparison of children 's levels of development and an assessment based on age-related developmental norms and milestones.

1.2 Child observation practices in German day care centres

Apart from these more general attitudinal aspects, there is no tradition of child monitoring and to date German practitioners are not pressured to track and report regularly on children 's development or progress.

What does observational practice look like in the day care centres? Our study shows:

- the method of child observation that is most familiar to practitioners is the unstructured observation of the whole child
- the observation of specific domains (e.g. language) on the basis of structured observation schemes is the exception
- many observations are not documented
- the most common form of documentation are informal, hand-written notes, run-on narratives about the observed situation or child
- in general children are not observed regularly, but rather for specific occasions
- (e.g. before meetings with parents, some months before school entry)

- systematic observation is often reserved for children with behavioural or developmental problems
- both systematic and spontaneous observations tend to focus on children 's social behaviour

Some disadvantages of this predominantly unstructured observation and documentation scheme are:

- it is time-consuming and as a rule not all children are observed regularly
- it will not allow for a comparison of children
- it does not provide a systematic record of a child's developmental processes
- narrative notes are difficult to interpret and are not useful for planning a curriculum
- unstructured observations and run-on notes cannot be easily shared with colleagues

Given this state of affairs, an important part of our in-service training for the implementation of the involvement scales was to discuss with the practitioners their habits, their attitudes and their practices in child observation and assessment – and we believe this should, in general, be an important aspect of all projects concerned with introducing and implementing specific observation schemes. In our case it gave practitioners a chance, not only to learn about the concept of involvement and the use of the involvement scales but also to reflect on their own observational and educational practice. This complex process – reflecting generally accepted professional ideals and habits and at the same time learning a new approach – was, for the majority of practitioners in our study an eye-opener. Most of them were very enthusiastic about the whole project. Nevertheless, without our ongoing monitoring process many practitioners (we were told) would have "fallen back" and resumed old habits, in spite of their views that they had learned to use a very rewarding, and child-centred approach. Using a process of child observation and assessment during a specific action research project is not the same as using it in everyday practice – without a support system.

2 Theoretical and methodological questions

Now our frame of reference is not so much early childhood culture but rather the scientific community. Involvement as it is used here has been extensively described in previous publications by Laevers and colleagues (e.g. Laevers, 1994a, pp.4-7; Laevers, 1994b, pp. 162-164). How is the concept of involvement connected to other theories?

2.1 Involvement and related concepts

Laevers' main points of reference are: Gendlin's concept of "experience" (e.g. Laevers 1994b, p.171) and Csikszentmihayli's concept of "flow". The concept of flow appears to be especially relevant for an understanding of involvement. Flow describes a specific type of subjective and immediate experience related to an activity. Flow is an autotelic experience characterised by (a) enjoyment, (b) holistic feelings of being immersed in, and of being carried by an activity, (c) merging of action and awareness, (d) concentration on the task at hand, (e) loss of self-consciousness combined with a very active role of the self, (f) sense of control of ones actions and the environment, (g) clear goals and immediate feedback (Csikszentmihayli, 1990). Many characteristics of flow also apply to involvement, and Laevers actually describes involvement as an experience of flow. However, unlike flow, the concept of involvement does not merely address the subjective experience related to an activity, but also the quality of the activity itself.

We would like to mention a few additional points of reference which may help to locate involvement and its various dimensions on the vast map of motivational theory and applied research.

First of all involvement is clearly related to theories of *intrinsic motivation* (e.g. Eccles, Wigfield & Schiefele, 1998). When individuals are intrinsically motivated they do activities for their own sake, out of interest in the activity itself, and not for instrumental reasons or any other reason such as social acceptance. Self-determination is a key concept in both intrinsic motivation and involvement and it has often been used to differentiate between intrinsic and extrinsic motivation. However, extrinsically motivated activities vary in the extent to which they can become self-determined activities – when external regulation is transformed into internal regulation (Deci, 1992, p. 54). Concerning involvement, it is clear that high involvement in a teacher-directed activity means that the activity has been transformed by the child into a personally meaningful and interesting event.

Closely related to the notion of intrinsic motivation is the concept of interest (e.g. Renninger, Hidi & Krapp, 1992). Interest theory has not merely focused on individual relatively stable interest domains, but also on task-oriented situational interest and the latter is closely related to the concept of involvement. In situational interest it is the relation between person and object, the feelings and values associated with an object that count. The same applies to the concept of involvement, but this concept puts greater emphasis on the emotion and energy attached to an activity and on the quality of the activity as it is performed by the child.

A third concept which seems important for an understanding of involvement is exploration (Berlyne, 1960). Exploration is taken to be a basic human need and drive, enhancing development and increasing an individual' s competence. An activity involving exploration means that specific characteristics of a process or an object are being observed, explored and manipulated, which are not hitherto known to the exploring individual. Thus the term is used to describe activities that go beyond routine and involve self-determined expeditions into the unknown. These activities are usually intrinsically motivated and accompanied by pleasure, and they are often associated with a child' s play. For educational settings a key question of quality has been whether the environment is rich and inspiring, whether it provides ample opportunities for the child to "explore".

Apart from these more general motivation theories involvement can also be related to concepts developed in applied research. Two specific concepts, both developed in empirical research on child development, have great affinity with involvement: "task orientation" and "engagement". Task orientation has come to be a classic empirically derived dimension in many child assessment instruments. It is often used in different areas of practice and research and has been widely acknowledged as a key factor for assessing and predicting child development and adaptation to educational settings and demands (e.g. Mayr, 2000; Mobley & Pullis, 1991). Salient factors are (task) persistence and distractibility (i.e. concentration). This is commonly operationalized in terms of time spent on task, completion of task, mastering of obstacles, concentration. Persistence and concentration are also key indicators of involvement. However, unlike task persistence, involvement also addresses the subjective and affective value of an activity for the child, the child' s emotional and cognitive "investment". Moreover the emphasis is less on the completion of a task than on the complexity and exploratory dimensions of task performance. Similar to involvement is the concept of engagement as used by McWilliam and colleagues (McWilliam, 1991; McWilliam & Bailey, 1995; de Kruif & McWilliam, 1999). It focuses on the quality of children' s engagement and, unlike mastery-motivation, it also includes less goal-directed behaviours. It is described with behaviours such as pretend play, persistence, attention, participation. Similar to the work on involvement, the Children' s Engagement Questionnaire (McWilliam, 1991) also addresses the issue of complexity, exploration and developmental level of a child' s activity. However, unlike involvement, the concept of engagement was developed in the traditional mode of empirical research with factor- and item-based observation and assessment scales (the same applies to task orientation).

2.2 The involvement scales as a tool for practitioners

As mentioned before, the primary purpose of the involvement training package was to improve the quality of early years' educational practice – by enhancing professional development and centre-based quality development. The observation scales are meant to be used primarily by early years' teachers. This frame of reference is important for an understanding of the characteristic features of the concept of involvement and of the involvement scales.

One of the outstanding characteristics of this approach is that several dimensions from different research traditions and theories are gathered into a single concept addressing motivational, emotional and cognitive aspects of a child's activity. Moreover the concept combines a well-accepted observational category like "task orientation" with dimensions that demand both observational and interpretative competence operating simultaneously at two different levels: (a) the observer must reconstruct the child's perspective during an activity (intrinsic motivation, enjoyment, the emotional value of an activity, the intensity of the experience), and (b) he/she must assess the level at which the child is operating (is the task challenging for the child, is the child exploring, trying out something new, is the activity relatively complex for this specific age group?). These diverse aspects of involvement - ranging form task persistence to the "felt meaning " of an experience - are singled out and discussed during the video training, but for the actual observation and assessment of children they are "reunited" under a single concept, the child's involvement. The complexity of the term "involvement" is paralleled by a relatively complex scaling procedure, where each point of the scale addresses different dimensions of an activity simultaneously. It ranges from level one, where "there is no real activity, the child is mentally absent" to level 5 with its sustained and intense activity requiring mental effort, showing concentration, persistence, energy, total immersion, and complexity.

Obviously, such an observation and assessment procedure and tool raises some theoretical problems and it is unusual in research contexts. At the same time it also has several advantages – all related to its application and applicability in day care centres.

31

2.2.1 COMBINING A HOLISTIC PERSPECTIVE WITH SYSTEMATIC OBSERVATION

As mentioned before our study in German day care centres (Ulich & Mayr, 1999a) revealed that practitioners' observation practice is generally guided by a holistic ideal: the child should be regarded as a complex entity, it should not be pinned down and labelled with a single aspect of its behaviour. To a certain extent, the concept of involvement allows practitioners to remain in this holistic mode, as it makes them look at the child 's activity as a whole. At the same time the involvement training program does teach practitioners to isolate different aspects of the child 's activity and to observe systematically, so that the subjective meaningfulness of the observation procedure is combined with a learning experience encouraging more systematic and more valid observation and assessment.

2.2.2 A "USER-FRIENDLY" TOOL

The involvement scales are relatively short and easy to handle. Both these characteristics are important for scales that are meant to be used by practitioners in their daily practice – cf. Schweinhart's comments on "user-friendly" observation tools (Schweinhart, 1993, p.30). An alternative would be to differentiate the emotional, cognitive and motivational levels of a child 's activity into various dimensions and corresponding items. This would entail more time-consuming observation and assessment tools that might be difficult for practitioners to use in everyday practice.

2.2.3 AN EXERCISE IN EMPATHY

This type of observation encourages practitioners to reconstruct the child 's perspective during an activity. Even though a child 's involvement can be observed and assessed on the basis of several behavioural indicators, the observer is required to register more than overt behaviour, she/he must also infer what the activity actually means for the child. This interpretative process encourages practitioners to look beyond a child 's actions and to search for cues telling them what the child is actually feeling and experiencing during an activity - an "exercise in empathy".

3 The Involvement Activities Scale as an instrument for centre-based quality development

Of special interest for our purpose was the "educational" orientation of the involvement scales. While most child observation scales are differentiated along developmental domains (language, motor skills, social competence, etc), in this case the focus of observation is a child' s behaviour in relation to specific curriculum activities within the day care centre. Observing a child`s level of involvement during a specific activity does not only tell practitioners about a child`s individual interests. When a child does not get involved during a picture-book reading session this may also reflect on the way the picture book is being presented. Thus, this type of observation can be related to the curriculum, to the way the activity is being offered within the educational setting.

This applies especially to the so-called Involvement Activities Scale (Laevers et al., 1996). Thus our study focused on the implementation of this specific scale (Mayr & Ulich, 1999; Ulich & Mayr, in press)

3.1 Procedure

The project introduced the concept of involvement and the Leuven involvement scales in German day care centres in a context of collaborative research. To test its general applicability a heterogeneous sample of day care centres was selected, with a total of 8 centres and 28 classes. 625 children were observed with the Activities Scale. The sample consisted of children from 3 to 7 years old, 9.3% of the children were of non-German nationality or they had families who had migrated to Germany (as foreigners or as "Aussiedler", i.e. German immigrants from Eastern Europe).

With the Involvement Activities Scale an individual child 's involvement is assessed for a whole range of different activities. The scale lists a total of 23 different activities - for some points the original list from Flanders was modified to suit German kindergarten practice (table 1).

Table 1: List of activities on the "Activities Scale" (version used in this study)

Physical activities	Small construction material	Picture books
Moulding, modelling	Board and card games	Stories
Water; sand	Puzzle, educational games	Listening to music
Drawing, colouring, painting	Work sheets	Making music
Scissoring, gluing, folding	Concepts of time, space, maths	Routine activities
Hammering, wood work	Role play	Excursions
Discovery table, technical instruments	Acting	Animals and plants
Big construction material	Group discussions	

Each activity is described with several examples on an additional sheet. This list of activities is meant to cover the whole range of curricular activities which normally occur in kindergarten. Class teachers were free to add special activities

33

that were not mentioned on the list. For each activity teachers rated the level of involvement on a five-point rating scale. The period of observation was 6 - 8 weeks. During this time every child in class was observed and assessed with the Activities Scale. All practitioners participating in the study (N=67) received an intensive training prior to their assessment of children with the Activities Scale.

All children participating in the study were observed and assessed on the basis of this scale by the two practitioners working in that class – in most cases one educator ("Erzieherin") and one nursery worker ("Kinderpflegerin"). Each practitioner observed and assessed approximately half of the children in class, so that each had 10 - 13 children to observe for a period of 6 - 8 weeks.

4 Findings

The Activities Scale tells a practitioner a lot about an individual child – in relation to curriculum activities. At the same time it may also be used to investigate more general aspects of quality: when practitioners apply the scale to all children in class, they are in a position to compare different groups of children – e.g. boys and girls – in their reactions to specific curriculum activities. It is this more general level of analysis that is the focus of the present study. We investigated the potential of the Child Involvement Activities Scale for highlighting issues of quality development relating to the developmental chances of different groups of children (for a more detailed presentation of our findings see Ulich & Mayr, in press).

Three groups will be discussed: (a) girls and boys, (b) ethnic minority children as compared to German children, (c) children of different ages. Looking at these groups we were interested in both the general level of involvement and in the level of involvement for each activity. In order to analyse the general level of involvement a total involvement score (TI) for each child was computed: the sum of a child' s involvement scores on all activities that had been assessed for that child was divided by that same number of activities.

4.1 Girls and boys

What does the Activities Scale tell us about gender-based involvement trends and activity preferences? Within the day care centres, the mean level of involvement (TI) was the same for boys and girls. However, this result does not imply that they have the same activity preferences. Significant differences between boys and girls were found for 16 out of 23 different activities. Boys show higher involvement rates in: "physical activities", "water, sand", "hammering, wood work", "discovery tables, technical instruments", "large construction material" and "small construction material". Girls` involvement rates are higher than boys` in: "moulding, modelling", "drawing, painting", "scissoring, gluing, folding", "board and card games", "puzzle, educational games", "work sheets", "role play", "acting", "listening to music", "routine

Figure 1: Activities in which girls have significantly higher involvement rates. Mean ranks per activity

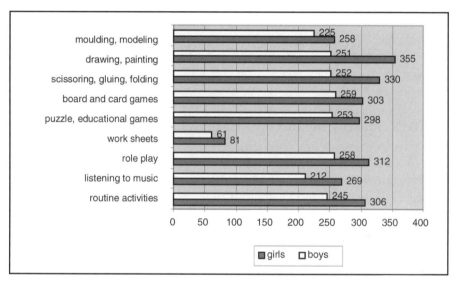

Figure 2: Activities in which boys have significantly higher involvement rates. Mean ranks per activity

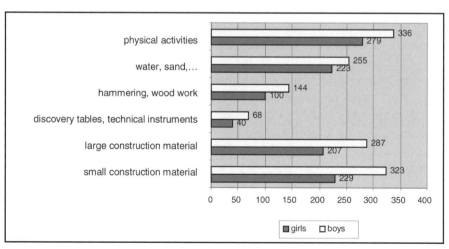

activities". Clearly, these are gender-stereotyped preferences: girls favour more sedentary, language-related and "school-oriented" activities, whereas boys prefer more expansive and manual/technical activities.

These findings indicate that boys and girls tend to live in different worlds not only in their social interactions but also in their curriculum activities, in their learning experiences. Previous studies – with different methods – have come to similar conclusions (e.g. Martin, Eisenbud & Rose, 1995; Roopnarine, 1984; Serbin & Sprafkin, 1986). In a recent study Laevers and Verboven (2000) showed that the "gender sensitivity" of childrens` activities is to some extent affected by the educational style of day care centres. Conceptualising the development of gender schemas as a process of self-socialisation in day care centres (e.g. Marhall, Robeson & Keefe, 1999; White, 1998) gives special significance to boys` and girls` involvement in different curriculum activities as part of this process.

4.2 Ethnic minority children – German children

How does early childhood education enhance the school-based and developmental competence of minority children? Significant differences between German and ethnic minority children were found for the Total Involvement scores on the Activities Scale, which means that, on the whole, ethnic minority children in day care centres have a lower level of involvement than German children. Testing the effect of ethnicity for each activity on the Activities Scale revealed significant differences for 4 curriculum activities: "role play", "group discussions", "picture books", "stories" - all of them language and literacy-related activities. In other words: language minority children, who have to cope with a relatively complex bilingual or multilingual developmental task, and who are expected to learn a second language (German) in pre-school do not fully participate in language and literacy related activities. These are precisely those activities that would be most important for their language development as they foster vocabulary development and expressive language skills (e.g. Hargrave & Sénéchal, 2000; Lonigan & Whitehurst, 1998); moreover literacy-related activities (story telling and shared book reading) would encourage children to go beyond conversational language usage and learn about the negotiation and collaborative construction of meaning, about de-contextualized and symbolic use of language - a prerequisite of "academic language" usage (e.g. Wells, Barnes & Wells, 1984; Whitehead, 1994; Whitehurst & Lonigan, 1998). These findings – together with the ratings mentioned above - raise some serious questions concerning a developmentally appropriate language and literacy curriculum for minority children in German day care centres.

4.3 Different age-groups

Unlike in some other European countries such as France or Belgium, in most German day care centres children of different ages are grouped together (Oberhuemer & Ulich, 1997). In our sample the age range was 3 - 6, with a few 7-year-olds.

According to our findings the level of children 's involvement rises proportionately with the age. This applies to children 's Total Involvement score as well as to the different curriculum activities. Out of 23 activities, there were no age effects for merely 3 activities. The difference of children 's Total Involvement scores between 3- and 6/7-year olds is remarkable: almost a whole point on the 5-point raring scale.

How are these findings to be interpreted? To see this as an argument in favour of age-homogeneous groups, would be misleading, as we did not make a comparison of children in age-homogeneous and age-heterogeneous groups. Nevertheless, the relatively low involvement rates of 3- and 4-year olds do open up some questions: e.g. how could an individualised age-appropriate curriculum guarantee higher involvement rates in younger children, or: would younger children's development in some areas be enhanced by age-homogeneous groups? Such questions should be pursued in further studies.

In any case, the results of the present study indicate that, as Freedman (1982, p. 205) pointed out almost 20 years ago, practitioners in age-mixed groups should monitor children's development with special care – this applies to younger children as well, and not merely, as has often been proposed, to older children.

Apart from this developmental dimension, these findings also raise a methodological question. In his instructions Laevers (1994a) indicates that practitioners, in order to assess a child's involvement rate, they should relate the quality of the activity to the developmental level of that child's age group. In principle, there should really be no systematic age-differences in involvement. However, our findings indicate that practitioners did not in fact apply this "implicit age norm". Possibly this type of "age biased" assessment does not surface in age-homogeneous groupings (such as in Belgium or France). Should this "bias" be confirmed by further studies, a child' s level of involvement in age-mixed groups would have to be related to age norms.

5 Conclusion

International co-operation leading to transcultural implementation of educational concepts and methods opens up many new perspectives and raises some interesting questions on various levels of implementation. In any case, such a process of migration should refer to the specific educational culture of the "receiving country" – taking into account the educational system, practitioners `attitudes, and professional values in the field. This article describes our experiences in introducing and implementing involvement as a concept and observation method in German early childhood education.

Looking back, we would like to conclude: The concept of involvement is immediately appealing to German practitioners and it fits well into the German educational culture. However, regular and systematic child observation with the involvement scales is a different story. In an early childhood culture where systematic child observation and documentation is unusual it is difficult for practitioners to sustain their motivation for this type of "extra work" during everyday practice. For such an activity to be transformed from "extra work" to "normal work" would require fundamental changes in German educational culture and professional values. Current discussions on quality development in German early childhood education may trigger off some changes – but that will take time.

On a different level such a process of transcultural migration means placing the new concept and approach within the international scientific community and discussing it in the context of related, well-established concepts and research activities, e.g. "intrinsic motivation", "interest", "exploration", "task persistence", "engagement".

Finally our empirical research yielded some interesting results pertaining to quality development: practitioners' observation and assessment of over 600 children with the Involvement Activities Scale showed that, generally speaking, different groups of children – girls and boys, ethnic minority children, younger children - do not have the same developmental chances in day care centres. The observation of children with the Involvement Activities Scale leads to substantial and differentiated information on specific dimensions of educational quality in day care centres – on a very practical and centre-based level. These findings may also be relevant for early childhood settings in other countries and cultures.

References

Berlyne, D. E. (1960). *Conflict, arousal and curiosity.* New York: McGraw Hill.

Csikszentmihayli, M. (1990). *Flow – the psychology of optimal experience.* New York: Harper & Row.

Deci, E. L. (1992). The Relation of interest to the motivation of behaviour: A self-determination theory perspective. In K. A. Renninger, S. Hidi & A. Krapp (Eds.), *The role of interest in learning and development* (pp. 43-70). Hillsdale: Lawrence Erlbaum.

Eccles, J. S., Wigfield, A. & Schiefele, U. (1998). Motivation to succeed. In W. Damon & N. Eisenberg (Eds.), *Handbook of child psychology, volume 3* (pp. 1017-1095). New York: John Wiley.

Freedman, P. (1982). A comparison of multi-age and homogeneous age grouping in early childhood centers. In L. G. Katz (Ed.), *Current topics in early childhood education* (pp. 193–211). Norwood: Ablex Publishing Corporation.

Hargrave, A. C. & Sénéchal, M. (2000). A book reading intervention with preschool children who have limited vocabularies: The benefits of regular reading and dialogic reading. *Early Childhood Research Quarterly, 15,* 75-90.

De Kruif, R. E. L. & Mc William, R. A. (1999). Multivariate relationships among developmental age, global engagement, and observed child engagement. *Early Childhood Research Quarterly 14,* 515-536.

Laevers, F. ,et al. (1994a). *The Leuven Involvement Scale for Young Children* [manual and videotape]. Leuven: Centre for Experiential Education.

Laevers, F. (1994b). The innovative project "Experiential Education" and the definition of quality in education. In F. Laevers (Ed.), *Defining and assessing quality in early childhood education* (pp.159-172). Leuven: Leuven University Press.

Laevers, F., Vandenbussche, E., Kog, M. & Depondt, L. (1996). *A process-oriented child monitoring system for young children.* Leuven: Centre for Experiential Education.

Laevers, F. & Verboven, L. (2000). Gender related role patterns in preschool settings. Can "experiential education" make a difference? *European Early Childhood Education Research Journal, 8,* 25-42.

Lonigan, C. J. & Whitehurst, G. J. (1998). Relative efficacy of parent and teacher involvement in shared-reading intervention for preschool children from low-income backgrounds. *Early childhood Research Quarterly, 13,* 263-290.

Marshall, N. L., Robeson, W. W. & Keefe, N. (1999). Gender equity in early childhood education. *Young Children, 54*, 9–13.

Martin, C. L., Eisenbud, L. & Rose, H. (1995). Children's gender–based reasoning about toys. *Child Development, 66*, 1453–1471.

Mayr, T. (2000). Beobachtungsbogen für Kinder im Vorschulalter (BBK) – ein Vorschlag zu Skalenbildung. *Psychologie in Erziehung und Unterricht, 47*, 280–295.

Mayr, T. & Ulich, M. (1998). Kinder gezielt beobachten. Teil 1: Der Stellenwert von Beobachtung im Alltag. *KiTa aktuell (BY), 10*, 205-209.

Mayr, T. & Ulich, M. (1999). Kinder gezielt beobachten. Teil 3: Die Engagiertheit von Kindern in Tageseinrichtungen. *KiTa aktuell (BY), 11*, 100- 105.

McWilliam, R. A. (1991). *Children's Engagement Questionnaire*. Chapel Hill, NC: Frank porter Graham Child Development Center, University of North Carolina at Chapel Hill.

McWilliam, R. A. & Bailey, Jr., D. B. (1995). Effects of classroom social structure and disability on engagement. *Topics in Early Childhood Special Education, 15*, 123-147.

Mobley, C. E. & Pullis, M. E. (1991). Temperament and behavioral adjustment in preschool children. *Early Childhood Research Quarterly, 6*, 577-586.

Oberhuemer, P. & Ulich, M. (1997). *Working with young children in Europe. Provision and staff training*. London: Paul Chapman.

Renninger, K. A., Hidi, S. & Krapp, A. (Eds.) (1992). *The role of interest in learning and development*. Hillsdale: Lawrence Erlbaum.

Roopnarine, J. E. (1984). Sex-typed socialization in mixed-aged preschool classrooms. *Child Development, 55*, 1078-1084.

Schweinhart, L. J. (1993). Observing young children in action: The key to early childhood assessment. *Young Children, 48* (5), 29-33.

Serbin, L. A. & Sprafkin, C. (1986). The salience of gender and the process of sex typing in three-to seven year old children. *Child Development, 57*, 1188-1199.

Ulich, M. & Mayr, T. (in press). *Children's involvement profiles in German day care centers*.

Ulich, M. & Mayr, T. (1999a). Observing children in German daycare centres.

Practitioners' attitudes and practice. *International Journal of Early Years Education,* *7,* 25-37.

Ulich, M. & Mayr, T. (1999b). Beobachtung und Professionalität. In H. Colberg-Schrader, D. Engelhard, D. Höltershinken, K. Neumann, T. Sprey-Wessing (Eds.), *Kinder in Tageseinrichtungen. Ein Handbuch für Erzieherinnen* (pp. 375-381). Seelze-Velber: Kallmeyersche Verlagsbuchhandlung.

Wells, G., Barnes S. & Wells, J. (1984). *Linguistic influences on educational attainment.* Bristol: University of Bristol.

White, M. (1998). "The pink`s run out!" The place of artmaking in young children`s construction of the gendered self. In N. Yelland (Ed.), *Gender in early childhood* (pp. 223-248). London: Routledge.

Whitehead, M. (1994). *Language and literacy in the early years* (2nd ed.). London: Paul Chapman.

Whitehurst, G. J. & Lonigan, C. J. (1998). Child development and emergent literacy. *Child Development, 69,* 848-872.

Improving the quality of early childhood education from "within"

Maria Nabuco, Silvério Prates

1 Introduction

Teachers have to make decisions about the kinds of procedures to adopt in order to improve the quality of the nursery settings. How can self-evaluation help them to have greater impact and at the same time improve children's "well-being"?

This article will present and examine a project in which 37 nursery teachers were involved, in three clusters of 37 classes spread over three different areas of Portugal, (Northern Coastal, Central Inland and Central Coastal). They carried out self-evaluations and took initiatives to improve the quality of the environment over one school year. The main goal of this project is to implement a strategy to support the development of quality in the settings, in the context of the in-service-training of 9 Early Years Advisers and that from the start ECERS-R (Harms, Clifford and Cryer, 1998) was selected both as the instrument to support the teachers and measure the increase in quality.

According to Epstein (1993), in-service training has to be carried out and available in the setting. This training is much more effective when the advisers know the settings, the children and the surrounding community. Another important consideration is that in-service training "should be continuous and constant (p.13)". The best in-service training lays emphasis on learning as an active and interactive process rather than as passive and reactive. It stresses individual support for learners, and responsiveness to the range of differences in characteristics and needs of the trainees. From Epstein's study it is also possible to conclude that in-service training can contribute significantly to the quality of the programme and child development.

Teachers, according to Harms (1990) have the possibility to assess various components of quality, through questionnaires completed by parents, by record keeping and through interviews of other staff members. "But it is only through observation of children and staff as they function in a setting, that it is possible to judge the implementation of the curriculum, the tone of the interpersonal interactions, and the responsiveness of the physical environment (p.65)." Harms pointed to observation as the basis for evaluating the environment, just as the High/Scope Foundation also pointed to observation as the best way of assessing both the environment and the development of the child. Harms published in 1998 the Early Child Environment Rating Scale-Revised Edition (ECERS-R) to evaluate the environment of pre-school settings.

Two new observational instruments for early childhood education have emerged. These are The Leuven Involvement Scale for Young Children (LIS-YC) by Laevers (1994b), to evaluate the quality of the involvement of each child in play or task activities, and the Adult Engagement Scale by Pascal, Bertram & Ramsden (1994), to evaluate teacher engagement. This scale is based on the Adult Style Observation Schedule (Laevers, 1993).

The ECERS-R scale will be considered in this article as a useful tool to evaluate the quality of environment of the programmes being offered in nursery schools in Portugal. The Leuven Involvement Scale for Young Children (LIS-YC) will also be considered as an instrument to see whether the quality of the environment has any impact on the "well-being" of the children.

2 The Early Childhood Environment Rating Scale (ECERS)

One of the most commonly used scales for research purposes around the world is the Early Childhood Environment Rating Scale (ECERS) developed by Harms, Clifford and Cryer (1980). This scale makes it possible to look at each setting in terms of the quality of the environment being provided. It has been used for research purposes always supplemented by other instruments. From our point of view ECERS is important for planning improvements through evaluation and also through nursery teachers' self-evaluation.

The ECERS (1980) was criticised by Statham and Brophy (1992). They described a study of playgroups in England, which used the ECERS. They pointed to certain 'difficulties and problems using it' in the playgroup context, but they also added that 'this is not to say that the scale had no value or was completely inappropriate as a means of assessing the playgroup environment. In fact it proved a useful tool for structuring observations'. However, they suggested certain modifications. The main modifications were related to the Playgroups Philosophy.

According to Statham and Brophy (1992) ECERS is based on a philosophy of direct learning; the Playgroups Association lays the emphasis on the child learning through free play, sometimes extended by adults, but initiated by the child. Parental involvement was another area, targeted by the playgroups but not covered in depth. Statham and Brophy suggested an additional scale for parental involvement. The short opening hours of Playgroups was another feature that made certain items inappropriate, i.e. 'personal grooming', 'space for nap or rest' and 'balanced diet' could not be applied easily to playgroups. Other criteria such as 'used weekly' or 'available every morning' were also difficult to apply because some Playgroups are not open throughout the week. These were the main items that presented difficulty in using ECERS in the playgroups context because of a different values base or operating schedule.

At the same time there are other items that Statham and Brophy felt should be supplemented by additional instruments. These are the items related with 'culture awareness', which from Statham and Brophy's (1992) point of view are treated superficially, as are the relationships between adults and children or between children and their peers. In order to overcome the problems pointed out by Statham and Brophy, other researchers have supplemented ECERS with other types of observation such as those used by Phillips, McCartney and Scarr (1987) or Whitebook, Howes and Phillips (1990). ECERS describes the environment very well, but does not describe the learning experience of individual children, as fully as many researchers would wish. For this reason ECERS should be complemented by systematic child observation or other kinds of rating scales.

Many of Statham and Brophy's (1992) criticisms are already covered by the ECERS-Revised version republished under the name Early Childhood Environment Rating Scale-Revised Edition (ECERS-R) by Harms, Clifford and Cryer (1998). According to the authors the ECERS-R is not a new scale, since it has the same rationale and underlying constructs. This revised version contains seven sub-scales and 43 items (Table 1) with each item expressed as a 7 – point scale with descriptors of 1 (inadequate), 3 (minimal), 5 (good), and 7 (excellent).

According to the authors, several changes have been made in the revised version. Some items have been combined to eliminate redundancy, while others have been expanded into separate items to deepen the content. Some items have been added for areas not covered in the ECERS. Indicators and examples have been added to many items to make them more inclusive and culturally sensitive. It is also possible with ECERS-R to mark Yes, No or NA (not applicable) for each indicator separately. This will help to identify more clearly the basis for the item quality score.

Reliability and validity have also been explored with the ECERS-R. The tests for this purpose were conducted in 45 classrooms. The authors were not satisfied with the inter-rate reliabilities obtained and decided that further revision was

Table 1: ECERS-R sub-scales and items

Sub-scales	Items
1. Space and Furnishing	Indoor space, furniture for routine care, play and learning, furnishing for relaxation and comfort, room arrangement for play, space for privacy, child-related display, space for gross motor play, gross motor equipment.
2. Personal Care and Routines	Greeting/departing, meals/snacks, nap/rest, toileting/diapering, health practices, safety practices.
3. Language Reasoning	Books and pictures, encouraging children to communicate, using language to develop reasoning skills, informal use of language.
4. Activities	Fine motor, art, music/movement, blocks, sand/water, dramatic play, nature/science, maths/number, use of TV, video, and/or computer, promoting acceptance of diversity.
5. Interaction	Supervision of gross motor activities, General supervision of children (other than gross motor), discipline, staff-child interactions, interactions among children.
6. Program Structure	Schedule, free play group time, provisions for children with disabilities
7. Parents and Staff	Provision for parents, provision for personal needs of staff, provision for professional needs of staff, staff interaction and co-operation, supervision and evaluation of staff, opportunities for professional growth.

needed. After the revisions, a second test was conducted on a sample of 21 classrooms. The percentage of agreement across the full 470 indicators in the scale was 81.1%, with no item having an indicator agreement level below 70%. At the item level, the proportion of agreement was 48% for exact agreement and 71% for agreement within one point. The authors also examined the internal consistency of the scale at the sub-scale and total score level. Sub-scale internal consistencies measured by Kappa ranged from .71 to .88 with a total scale internal consistency of Kappa = .92. These levels of internal consistency indicate that the sub-scales and total scale can be considered to represent reasonable levels of internal agreement.

The ECERS has been widely used in many different countries and its authors have tested validity and measured reliability. This instrument proves to be reliable and valid for measuring the characteristics of early childhood environments. It is believed by researchers to constitute a good measure of quality of the environment provided for children in early childhood education (Howes, Phillips & Whitebook, 1992; Scarr, Eisenberg & Deater-Deckard, 1994; Kärrby & Giota, 1994; Kärrby, Giota, Sheridan & Ogefelt, 1995; Tietze, Cryer, Bairrão, Palacios & Wetzel, 1996; Sylva, Siraj-Blatchford, Melhuish, Sammons, Taggart, Evans, Dobson, Jeavons, Lewis, Morahan & Sadler, 1999). However, ECERS-R has been used more for research purposes than for the evaluation and assessment of practice by staff in early childhood settings.

3 The Leuven Involvement Scale for Young Children (LIS-YC)

This study also supplements ECERS-R with another observational instrument The Leuven Involvement Scale for Young Children (LIS-YC) by Laevers (1994) aiming to evaluate and compare the quality of the involvement of each child in the play or task activities with the quality being provided measured by ECERS-R.

The Leuven Involvement Scale for Young Children has developed with the Experiential Education project. Within this project the concept of "involvement" has been conceptualised as a measure of quality observable at all ages. The LIS-YC has two components. The first component is a list of "signals" or aspects of behaviour one can anchor for judging the involvement of each child. The second component is a 5-point scale to measure the involvement level for each child.

In order to be able to rate the LIS-YC scale it is very important to observe the signals of involvement. The signals are: concentration, energy, complexity and creativity, facial expression and posture, persistence, precision, reaction in time, verbal utterances and satisfaction. Each one of the signals has it rationale.

The LIS-YC scale is a five-point scale. Scale rate 1: no activity. A rating of 1 it is reserved for the moments when the child is considered in a situation of no activity. These are the moments when the child is "non-active". Scale rate 2: frequently interrupted activity. A rating of 2 is reserved for situations in which the child shows apparent activity or even lack of activity, or in a situation of more or less uninterrupted activity. Scale rate 3: more or less continuous activity. For a rating of 3 it is necessary to observe the child in more or less continuously engaged activity. Scale rate 4: activity with intense moments. For a rating of 4 it is important that the involvement is expressed in the signals for at least half of the observation time. Scale rate 5: sustained intense activity. For a rating of 5 it is necessary that the child be observed in maximum involvement. According to the author, this level requires the presence of the signals of concentration, persistence, energy and complexity.

The LIS-YC can be used within settings but also for the practice of students in pre-service teacher training. The scale can be administered by head teachers, educational advisors or by researchers in different age groups.

Reliability and validity have also been explored with the LIS-YC by its authors. Two trained observer's awarded 30 points in a real classroom situation. The inter-rate reliability measured by Spearman was = .90, which demonstrates very high correlation. This instrument has also been shown to be reliable and valid for measuring child involvement believed by researchers (e.g. Pascal & Bertram, 1994; Pascal, Bertram & Ramsden 1994; Pascal, Bertram, Ramsden, Georgeson, Saunders & Mould 1995; Laevers, 1995; Pascal & Bertram, 1997) to constitute a good measure of evaluation of the process of education in early childhood settings.

In this research the authors of this article used the LIS-YC. Before using it the authors had many training sessions with video and in real life situations such as classroom observations with another observer. With this observer the inter-rate reliability between the observers was obtained through Spearman's correlation coefficient, and the score was = .85.

4 Research design

The research was conducted in 37 nursery classes in three different districts of Portugal: 7 classes in the Northern Coastal, 24 classes in the Central Inland and 6 classes in the Central Coastal (Table 2). The Early Childhood Environment Rating Scale requires informal observation based on global observational judgements and interview with the teacher. The authors of this article trained Early Years Advisers to become observers with ECERS-R through video and in real classrooms. The inter-rate reliability was obtained in real classrooms. Prior to starting to observe in the classrooms selected for the reliability exercises, the Early Years Advisers (as observers), became familiar with the scale: firstly, by studying the items, discussing the problems and the meaning of each item; secondly, by observing and rating other classrooms until a good level of agreement was obtained. To ensure ECERS-R reliability in this study, the observers conducted a formal inter-rate testing with the authors. The inter-rate reliability between the observers was obtained through Spearman's correlation coefficient, which was calculated for the seven sub-scales. The scores were as follows: 1. Space and Furnishings = .100; 2. Personal Care Routines = .42; 3. Language-Reasoning = .82; 4. Activities = .94; 5. Interaction = .39; 6. Programme Structure = .52; 7. Parents and staff = .61. The rating was done in one class during a full day session followed by a further morning (to reduce the possible effect of atypical days) and an interview with the teacher. Some items, those that did not exist at the time in the classrooms and were not possible to observe, were excluded.

The observers were nine Early Years Advisers. These districts were chosen since one of the authors of this research was training Early Years Advisers for in-service training and supervision.

Table 2: ECERS-R Sample

	Northern Coastal	Central Inland	Central Coastal
Classes	7	24	6

As a first step in these three districts, the Early Years Advisers were trained to observe nursery classes with ECERS-R through video and in a real life situation. After the training period they went to do observation in classrooms with the teachers' permission. After this first observation they offered the ECERS-R to the nursery teachers, encouraging them to use it as a self-evaluation tool.

The Early Years Advisers also invited each nursery teacher to a meeting after they had had the opportunity to do the self-evaluation. The aim of this meeting was to compare the ratings of the scale by the nursery teacher with those of the Early Years Adviser. After the comparison, each made a plan of improvement (see Appendix). Following the improvement plan, the nursery teachers committed themselves to take initiatives to improve the quality of their practice according to their particular circumstances. Influencing factors were for instance, finance, the support and help from the heads and the local authorities or stakeholders, the availability of help from initial training students doing their practice with them.

During the last month of the year, after a six-month interval, the Early Years advisers returned to visit the nurseries and did another formal observation with ECERS-R scale to verify the initiatives taken by the teachers (the improvement plan).

Also during this last month of the year, one of the researchers chose the largest nursery school of the sample, with six classes, in the Central Coastal and made an observation with the LIS-YC in three of the six classes. She observed 18 children during periods of three minutes per day, for four days, mornings and afternoons, in a total of twelve minutes each. The children were randomly selected, six from each class. Of the eighteen children, nine were boys and nine were girls (Table 3).

Table 3: LIS-YC sample (Central Coastal)

	Class 1	Class 2	Class 3	Total
3 years old		3 girls 3 boys		
4 years old	3 girls 3 boys			
5 years old			3 girls 3 boys	
Total	6	6	6	18 Children

5 Results from the ECERS-R

Table 4 shows the total progress made in the quality of environment provided in each district, through the process of advisers encouraging nursery teachers to do self-evaluation in their classes. The Central Coastal sample (six classes) were those that had the highest mean levels of quality, measured with ECERS-R at the beginning of the year (mean = 5.95) and were also those that reached the highest quality level at the end of the year (mean = 6.26). However, the improvement was 0.31. The lowest level at the beginning of the year was reached by the Central Inland sample (24 classes). The mean of this district at the starting point was 4.31 and at the end 4.50 the difference being 0.19. It was the district with the lowest level of quality improvement. The Northern Coastal district sample (7 classes) started with the mean = 4.7 and reached the mean = 5.23, reaching the highest level of improvement 0.53.

Table 4 shows the total ECERS-R scores by district, the total items coded, the mean ECERS-R scores, the number of classes observed and also the mean total at the start and at the end of the year. From these details, the progress over the year in each district can be seen.

Tables 5, 6 and 7 show the quality profiles at the starting point, at the end, and the progress over the year in each class. Table 4 demonstrates the progress of each class in the Northern Coastal. Which factors might have contributed to this improvement? Is it possible to explain this progress in terms of supervision and in-service training? In one sense it is possible that the supervision was the closest since the Early Year Advisers visited the settings four hours every three weeks and also had student teachers for the whole year. The Early Years

Table 4: ECERS-R scores by district

	Total ECERS Score	Total items coded	Mean ECERS-R scores	Number of classes Observed	Mean
Northern Coastal					
Start	1339	285	4.70	7	191.3
End	1497	286	5.23	7	213.9
Central Inland					
Start	3983	925	4.31	24	166.0
End	4158	925	4.50	24	173.3
Central Coastal					
Start	1445	243	5.95	6	240.8
End	1522	243	6.26	6	253.7

Advisers' decision was to involve these students in the self-evaluation and also in the improvement plan. It is therefore possible to look at this highest improvement from this angle. This group of teachers had the greatest support in putting the improvement plan into practice and were helped more than the others, not only by advisers, visiting them as it was pointed, during four hours every three weeks, but also by students.

Table 5: Northern Coastal – Total by classes

	Class 1	Class 2	Class 3	Class 4	Class 5	Class 6	Class 7
Start	5.07	4.73	4.90	3.81	3.95	5.19	5.21
End	5.84	4.85	5.16	4.05	4.15	6.31	6.14
Progress	0.77	0.13	0.27	0.24	0.21	1.12	0.93

Table 6 shows the progress over the year of 24 classes in the Central Inland district. Only three classes in the sample of this district made no progress.

Table 6: Central Inland – Total by classes

	Class 1	Class 2	Class 3	Class 4	Class 5	Class 6	Class 7	Class 8
Start	4.35	4.38	4.75	3.93	3.81	2.73	4.44	4.00
End	4.48	4.53	4.88	4.10	4.65	3.27	4.51	4.03
Progress	0.13	0.15	0.13	0.17	0.84	0.55	0.08	0.03

Table 6: Central Inland – Total by classes (cont.)

	Class 9	Class 10	Class 11	Class 12	Class 13	Class 14	Class 15
Start	4.41	4.76	3.59	2.10	4.63	4.95	4.75
End	4.51	5.08	3.59	2.13	4.97	5.23	5.00
Progress	0.10	0.32	0.00	0.03	0.34	0.28	0.25

Table 6: Central Inland – Total by classes (cont.)

	Class 17	Class 18	Class 19	Class 20	Class 21	Class 22	Class 23	Class 24
Start	4.53	4.82	3.57	4.87	5.41	5.25	4.00	4.21
End	4.78	5.26	3.57	5.00	5.49	5.30	4.00	4.33
Progress	0.25	0.45	0.00	0.13	0.08	0.05	0.00	0.13

Table 7 shows the progress made by the six classes from to the same nursery school in the Central Coastal district. All six classes made progress although they started high, were the ones with the highest level of quality, and were not the ones making highest progress over the six-month interval.

Table 7: Central Coastal – Total by classes

	Class 1	Class 2	Class 3	Class 4	Class 5	Class 6
Start	6.00	6.07	5.26	5.38	6.41	6.53
End	6.02	6.29	6.15	5.80	6.68	6.63
Progress	0.02	0.22	0.89	0.42	0.27	0.10

From a very detailed analysis of the results of the Central Inland district sample it is clear that although there was some improvement, (the mean = 4.495), after improvement does not reach the starting mean of the Northern Coastal sample (starting mean = 4.698). Looking at all the mean scores in the Central Inland sample, it was also clear that the sub-scale number 4 – Activities is the one with the largest progress (Table 8). This Table refers to the ECERS-R sub-scale number 4 related to the Nature and Science Activities of the curriculum. Observing Table 8 it is possible to see that ten classes made progress after six months of self-evaluation, and three at the starting point already had the maximum quality level, which was seven. What might explain this progress?

Table 8: Results of the Central Inland sample on Nature and Science

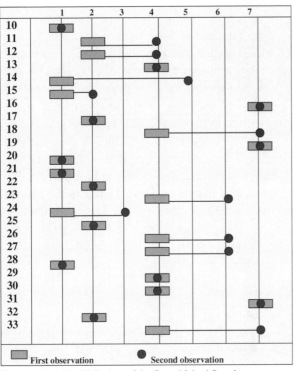

Numbers 10 to 33 – 24 Settings of the Central Inland Sample
Numbers 1-7 - ECERS-R Scores

It is again the closely-supervised in-service training in this area of knowledge (Nature and Science) together with the various workshops led by a Science Lecturer with nursery teachers who were involved and enjoying the partnership of this in-service training (28 hours divided by 7 sessions of 4 hours each) that led the classes to higher levels of quality.

6 Results from the LIS-YC

Figure 1 shows data from another instrument, the LIS-YC. The intention of using this instrument was to see whether it would be possible to compare the quality measured by ECERS-R with the involvement level measured by LIS-YC, with only three classes from to the same nursery school and with different homogeneous age groups of children. From the results, the conclusions are that the mean total for ECERS-R in this Class1 of 4-year-olds at the end of the year was 6.02 while in the LIS-YC the mean was 4.04 (Figure 1).

Figure 1: Class 1 (Central Coastal) - Mean = 4.04

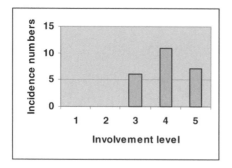

Figure 2 shows the LIS-YC results of class 2. The mean total for ECERS-R in this Class 2 of 3-year-olds at the end of the year was 6.29 while in the LIS-YC the mean was 3.96 (Figure 2).

Figure 2: Class 2 (Central Coastal) - Mean = 3.96

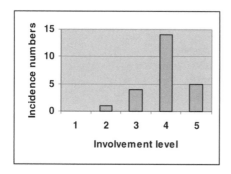

Figure 3 shows the LIS-YC results of Class 3. The mean total for ECERS-R in this Class 3 of 5-year-olds at the end of the year was 6.15 while in the LIS-YC the mean was 4.33 (Figure 3).

Figure 3: Class 3 (Central Coastal) - Mean = 4.33

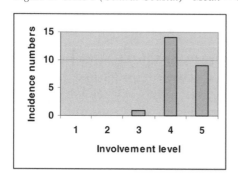

The conclusions are: for the ECERS-R the 3-year-olds where the ones that had the highest scores in quality of the environment, while in LIS-YC they had the lowest scores of involvement. The 5-year-olds did not have such high ECERS-R scores on quality of the environment but had the highest levels of involvement. From this result it is possible to conclude that in certain circumstances the 3-year-olds are not so deeply involved. It would be very interesting to compare the level of involvement of homogeneous classes of 3-year-olds by looking at the consistency of their results and comparing them with this small sample.

7 Discussion and conclusions

From the data described above of this exploratory research, it is clear that the strategies used in supervision and in-service training by the Early Years Advisers inviting nursery teachers to do self-evaluation with ECERS-R were important for quality improvement, as was the type of in-service training as partners with the Science lecturer. The level of improvement was clear in 34 classes; only 3 classes failed to make progress. Each nursery teacher made it clear that it was not possible to make more progress in some items, since this progress was not dependent on them but on decisions by school heads, local authorities or even stakeholders.

From a closer look at the results it is possible to note that the two sub-scales where progress were more evident was in sub-scale 1 – Space and furnishings and in sub-scale 4 – Activities. Why the larger progress in these two sub-scales? These two areas are those in which nursery teachers have the power to lead both the structure and the process. The first sub-scale is related to room arrangement for play, space for privacy and child-related display. These are areas where it is possible to act independently of the local authorities. Curriculum activities are another area of independence. Teachers in Portugal are free to draw up their own curriculum after looking at the Curriculum Guidelines published by the Ministry of Education. But these are only Guidelines; nursery teachers are free to decide curriculum issues for themselves.

It was not possible to compare children's involvement levels measured by the LIS-YC with the quality levels measured by ECERS-R. The conclusion from the LIS-YC observation results is that the older children were reaching higher levels of involvement.

There are several limitations to this study. The first is that the sample observed with the LIS-YC was too small to give the possibility of comparing the quality level with the involvement level. It would also be advisable to measure involvement in a pre-and post-test design like with the ECERS-R. A second fragile point is that the sample is not comparable from the outset since there were different class numbers in each district.

The strengths are the most important feature, and the main strength is that when in-service training and the supervision of the teachers is available in site, it is continuous and constant, and emphasizes learning as active and interactive rather than as passive and reactive can contribute significantly to programme quality and child development (Epstein, 1993). The settings which made higher progress in the Northern Coastal sample had four hours of supervision every three weeks and student teachers for the all year helping them to improve quality. The classes in the Central Inland sample which made more progress on Nature and Science had 28 hours of workshops lead by a Science Lecturer in site.

References

Bertram, T., Laevers, F. & Pascal, C. (1996). Étude de la qualité de l'interaction adulte-enfant dans le préscolaire: "le schéma d'observation du style de l'adulte". In S. Rayna, F. Laevers & M. Deleau (1996), *L'Éducation Préscolaire : quels objectifs pédago-giques?* (pp. 295 - 314). Baume-les-Dames: Nathan Pédagogie et INRP.

C.O.R. (1992). *Child Observation Record.* Ypsilanti, Michigan: High/Scope Press.

Epstein, A. S. (1993). *Training for quality. Improving early childhood programs through systematic inservice training.* Ypsilanti, Michigan: High/Scope Press.

Harms, T. (1990). The assessment of quality in child care settings. In T. Harms (Ed.), *Pre-school education meeting* (pp. 63-77). Lisboa: Fundação Calouste Gulbenkian. Serviço de Educação.

Harms, T., & Clifford, R. M. (Ed.) (1980). *Early Childhood Environment Rating Scale.* New York: Teachers College Press.

Harms, T., & Clifford, R. (1989). *Family Day Care Rating Scale.* New York: Teachers College Press.

Harms, T., Cryer, D., & Clifford, R. (1986). *Infant-Toddler Environment Rating Scale.* Chapel Hill: University of North Carolina.

Harms, T., Jacobs, E., & White, D. (Ed.) (1996). *School-Age Care Environment Rating Scale.* New York: Teachers College.

Harms, T., Clifford, R. M. & Cryer, D. (1998). *Early Childhood Environment Rating Scale* (Rev. ed.). New York: Teachers College Press.

Howes, C., Phillips, D. A., & Whitebook, M. (1992). Thresholds of quality: Implications for the social development of children in center-based child care. *Child Development, 63*, 449-460.

Kärrby, G., & Giota, J. (1994). Dimensions of quality in Swedish day care centers - An analysis of the early childhood environment rating scale. *Early Child development and Care, 104*, 1-22.

Kärrby, G., Giota, J., Sheridan, S., & Ogefelt, A. D. (1995). *Methods for evaluating the quality in pre-school: Research and developmental work* (Unpublished paper).

Laevers, F. (1993). Deep-level-learning. An exemplary application on the area of physical knowledge. *European Early Childhood Education Research Journal, 1*, 53-68.

Laevers, F. (1994a). The innovative project "Experiential Education" and definition of quality in early childhood education. In F. Laevers (Ed.), *Defining and assessing quality in early childhood education* (pp.159-172). Leuven: Leuven University Press.

Laevers, F. (1994b). *The Leuven Involvement Scale for Young Children* [manual and videotape]. Leuven: Centre for Experiential Education.

Laevers, F. (1995). *An exploration of the concept of involvement as an indicator for quality in early childhood care and education.* Dundee: Scottish CCC.

Pascal, C. & Bertram, T. (1994). Defining and assessing quality in the education of children from four to seven years. In F. Laevers (Ed.), *Defining and assessing the quality in early childhood education.* Leuven: Leuven University Press.

Pascal, C. & Betram, T. (1995). "Involvement" and the Effective Early Learning Project: A collaborative venture. In F. Laevers (1995). *An exploration of the concept of involvement as an indicator for quality in early childhood care and education* (pp. 22 –33). Dundee: Scottisch CCC.

Pascal, C. & Bertram, T. (1997). *Effective early learning. Case studies in improvement.* London: Hodder & Stoughton.

Pascal, C., Bertram, T. & Ramsden, F. (1994). *Effective early learning: The quality evaluation and development process.* Worcester: Amber Publications.

Pascal, C., Bertram, T., Ramsden, F., Georgeson, J., Saunders, M. & Mould, C. (1995). *Evaluating and developing quality in early childhood settings: A professional development programme.* Worcester: Amber Publications.

P.I.P (1989). *Program implementation profile.* Ypsilanti, Michigan: High/Scope Press.

Phillips, D. A., McCartney, K., & Scarr, S. (1987). Child care quality and children's social development. *Developmental Psychology, 23*, 537-543.

Scarr, S., Eisenberg, M., & Deater-Deckard, K. (1994). Measurement of quality in child care centers. *Early Childhood Research Quarterly, 9*, 131-151.

Statham, J., & Brophy, J. (1992). Using the 'Early Childhood Environment Rating Scale' in playgroups. *Educational Research, 34*, 141-148.

Sylva, K., Siraj-Blatchford, I., Melhuish, E., Sammons, P., Taggart, B., Evans, E., et al. (1999). *Technical paper 6. Characteristics of the centres in the EPPE sample: Observational profile. A longitudinal study funded by the DFEE 1997-2003.* London: University of London, Institute of Education.

Tietze, W., Cryer, D., Bairrão, J., Palácios, J. and Wetzel, G. (1996). Comparisons of observed process quality in early child care and education programs in five countries. *Early Childhood Research Quarterly, 11*, 447-475.

Whitebook, M., Howes, C. & Phillips, D. A. (1990). *Who cares? Child care teachers and the quality of care in America. The National Child Care Staffing Study.* Oakland: Child Care Employee Project.

Air-sea rescue terminated by lack of pedagogical tact:
A narrative account of the redeemed relationship between a researcher-artist-practitioner and her quarry
Diane Doble Leemans

1 Introduction

In this paper I want to share insights of an academic research process that struggled with the process of unveiling the secrets of the phenomenon of my research quarry and its essential realities, as well as the quest for an informing epistemological and methodological base. In my process as a researcher the breakthrough came when I began to get closer experientially to the phenomenon I observed; I allowed myself to see the phenomenon for itself, and to echo Heidegger's words, "let it show itself from itself (1962, p. 58)." I also began to recognise how instrumental the entries and 'process writing' in my work journals were. I realised how their interpretative writings offered a fruitful methodology and supported critical awareness in my quest for a refined re-search focus with developing intellectual rigour for meaningful, practical application. The interpretative text of my 'process writing' sought to develop a strong and oriented relation with the research and theorising. From them a human science perspective evolved that explores the relationship between pedagogical tact and the support of authentic expression in early childhood. It asserted itself as a phenomenological inquiry of 'lived experience' involving a philosophy in action in a pedagogic context.

Since I commenced my research I have held onto an imagining of the processes experienced by the sculptor, Michelangelo Buonarotti. He always tried to conceive his figures as lying hidden in the block of marble on which he was working; the undertaking he set himself was purely to remove the stone, which concealed them. He spent months at a time in the quarries of Carrara selecting blocks of marble that seemed to offer the promise of hidden forms. Employing mind, tools and methods Michelangelo pursued a developing relationship with the marble, working to deliver its essentiality and lucid design. I have used my understanding of this as a supportive analogy for the academic research process I am experiencing.

2 Air-sea rescue terminated by lack of pedagogical tact

A defining moment in my process as a researcher is well illustrated by an entry in one of my work journals. From amongst an accumulation of pieces of 'process writing' that served as a spur for affirmatively deciding upon my chosen research design, this one presented a cameo of an intensifying confidence in a particular research stance. Prior uncertainty concerning this was dissolved as I recognised some constant themes emerging from my writing. There was a fidelity to the manner in which I observed a pedagogical phenomenon, dwelt upon it and then explored through interpretative writing. The selected example commences with a title, which is reminiscent of a headline in a tabloid newspaper and designed to provoke further enquiry. It reads: 'Air-sea rescue terminated by lack of pedagogical tact: A reflective account by an observer at the early childhood scene of enactment'. In the terms of my work journal it served as an alarm heading for my pedagogic concerns, one that must be returned to for more profound interpretation. What lay behind this journalistic ploy to flag my attention for deeper reflection through interpretative writing, and now in this contribution, to hopefully draw the readers' attention, is an event that took place in an early childhood setting. It concerns a child engaged in a role-play activity involving an air-sea rescue. I recorded my observations on video and post hoc as a reflective narrative within a piece of 'process writing' in a work journal. I will describe this vignette later. For the moment I wish to hold the reader in a kind of suspense with an enticing overture. I aim to do this by suggesting that during this scene of role-play, those *in loco parentis*, through lack of pedagogical tact, unthinkingly terminated the activity. An awareness of the child's point of view and respect for the heightened sense of reality it must surely have encapsulated was absent. My interpretation of the event is that the abrupt cancellation of the child's role-play was tantamount to a 'real life' termination of an air-sea rescue, which if observed by a news reporter of a certain genre might well have instigated the attention seeking shock headline I have purposefully utilised.

2.1 An early childhood construal of the notion of diaries

As a child I was conditioned by the prevailing post 1939-45-war need to be materially thrifty. As children we were often usefully employed to slit open cartons, paper bags and envelopes so that we had paper for painting, model making, drawing and writing. It was an enjoyable activity, full of pent-up excitement for its potential uses. Sometimes we would assemble some of the opened sheets, fold them and sew them together to make books, or use cardboard to devise folders to keep less uniform sheets of paper together. When given a 'real' writing book - other than a school exercise one - or receiving a bought sketchbook, or diary it was treated with reverence. At the time the professional binding seemed to offer treasure chest security for one's contained written and visual describing. I longed for one of those diaries with a lock to fully endorse this sense. But sometimes I also found them awesome as if I should only use them when I felt in confident writing or drawing mood. The textural 'special ness' of their papers had an almost barring preciousness. I noticed that my parents and the adults around me wrote drafts and sketched out ideas on pieces of scrap paper that they transferred into folders, or pasted into their 'valuable' books as well as copying out some of them directly onto the bound paper. With pedagogical tact they encouraged me to overcome my tentativeness by doing likewise. They offered both flour and water paste and the idea that when you looked back at a sequence of such entries you could trace a process, keep or reject the ideas you felt were dissatisfactory and realise a journey of development that you owned. It was a rationale echoed by Eisner, when he spoke of the need to use our senses so that they actualise - possibly through language and images - rather than atrophy. With this encouragement to be confident about explicitly expressing the implicit he provided a balanced consideration of the personal utility of the product:

The development of competence is one of the major sources of self-satisfaction for children. None of us like to display our weaknesses and none of us like to remain at the same level of ability after substantial experience in a field of endeavour. The greatest spur to further work and to the setting of higher standards is the recognition that we have made progress. There is something we can do now that we couldn't do before (1979, p. 113).

I could explore both process and product of my creative acts within those bindings.

2.2 From diary to 'process writing'

Years later, on entering an art course in a secondary school and then a school of art I quickly noted with delighted surprise that embracing this way of working was a model expectation and the traditional tool of artists. As a theatre designer these writing/sketchbooks became indispensable. When I became professionally engaged with education this established habit continued in the same form but I began to call them work journals.
As a school-based artist-practitioner-researcher, and now as a university-based research student my work journals have continued. They still have uniform covers bulging with an accumulation of erratic-sized pages comprising:

63

conventional diary entries together with pasted, or attached related articles, photographs and visual image references, drawings, sketches and loose leaf hand-written, or word processed printouts of 'process writing'. By 'process writing' I mean personal thinking journeys through reflective writings that for example, commence as a counsel for my memory about events I have participated in, or observed in early childhood settings, whereupon they develop into construable searching. The purpose of 'process writing' is to potentially nurture and develop ideas. Like thought patterns, they sometimes flow but at other times they are amateurish and clumsy, or merely embryonic as I grapple to express the essence of an experience, give substance to a mere trace of an idea, or a fleeting memory that is in danger of losing its ephemeral form. A journal entry can look like a disjointed shape poem where representative words like an aspect of the concept of 'felt meanings' (Gendlin, 1964) drop onto the paper. These can be the sparks for 'process writing'.

Whatever enters a work journal has had a purpose, and is an expression and extension of my way of being, and responding to the 'lived experience' (van Manen, 1990,1991,1995) of early childhood matters, and working in the 'paradigm of noticing' (Mason, 1996) the phenomena of pedagogic life in those settings. Here, for example, was the opportunity, following a day of preliminary or pilot study activity, surrounded by young children not previously encountered, to plunge philosophically into the concepts of well-being, involvement, sensitivity and autonomy as developed by Laevers and colleagues (1993-2000). My explorations may be well-considered, inspirational expressions with structural clarity, or frustratingly tangled in a too hasty bid for meaning. They may be ramblings without a clear outcome, or they may have enthusiastically evolved and thrown up the surprise of, 'this is going somewhere', and 'I can develop this', or 'maybe this is worth sharing'. A work journal is for my purposes only; they are 'messages for myself'; my private accounts about the continuous act of becoming; my intellectual property.

I use work journals to record information, document events, note my responses and feelings toward my interactions with children, and express ideas and untangle puzzles. I have found, as Liz Jones (Jones, 2001) describes that they can support a journey to solve and release one from unhelpful habits and/or mechanistic practices. My work journals describe early childhood environments; their ambience: quality, smells, lighting, temperature, sound levels and so forth, as well as the processes being carried through there and products achieved. They become the store cupboard of ingredients for 'process writing' about post hoc reflections on past, 'just now' experiences, and future prospects and potentialities. As Dahlberg et al (1999), Rinaldi (1998) and atelierista,

64

Vera Vecchi (1998) have commented in similar vein - and I have since observed in some pre-schools, and baby and toddler centres of Reggio Emilia in Italy - work journals are an important instance of 'pedagogical documentation' to support self and the community's evaluation purposes. They can be a 'window' for parents to visualise their children's experience whilst *in loco parentis.*

Work journals have traced my research process, its problems and solutions. They record aspects of my preliminary studies where I have tracked my apprenticeship in developing research skills and compared this with approaches used previously as a teacher-researcher. I call these studies: 'research acquaintance with setting' and 'research technology acquaintance'. To explore the feasibility of proposed methods I have found it centring to use the vehicle of 'process writing' to evaluate their appropriateness.

3 'The road goes ever on': it is a process of self-awareness

Life can at times have episodes that are somewhat like a 'Lord of the Rings' (Tolkien, 1954/55) saga. It may be beset with trials and tribulations. In the struggle to hear one's inner voice there maybe pitfalls by ignoring its intuitive validity or attending to the direction it is offering, as well as joys and triumphs on reaching the high ground. Living my research studies has overtones of this kind of diversely patterned journey. Besides the literature, voices of experience come from many quarters advising this approach or that one, even skilful combinations of approach. Initially, it seemed like a minefield to me, in the middle of which lay my answers if only I could develop the question(s) to open an intelligent passage to seek them. This included the questions to be asked of more experienced informants. If one cannot communicate these effectively even the most patient person one is in dialogue with can be at a lost to fathom out what the trapped nuances of the concept the student is trying to gain ownership of may be. Sometimes I felt I was wandering in a wilderness and floundering around in dry pursuit of 'the supposed way of doing things'. This really was a metaphor for deafness to the inner voice and loss of confidence as I pursued a confused melange of perspectives that were inappropriate for handling the phenomena of an experiential approach. The work journals became a sounding board and a therapeutic tool for unravelling the muddled thinking I committed to its pages.

4 Realising one's voice was always there

It is a wise, tactful and tactical manoeuvre to advise a student that nobody knows more about this particular conceptual nugget being laboured over than the student herself. As I struggled with the domain of my research, it was suggested that the way of expressing it could be unique if I found my own voice to deliver it as a potential contribution to the larger body of knowledge. The sagacious emphasis on 'your own voice' was a decisive turning point in my studies as I realised that the unavoidable authenticity of the outpourings that went into my work journals was being ignored in my then research writing. I had forgotten to see these writings as an essential part of the overall research activity, a critical tool and instrument in the research process. By disregarding my own well-being and involvement I had overlooked the power that the experiential and process-oriented nature of using the work journals exercised. Ignoring their use was not idiosyncratic of the regard I had for them during school-based practices. It was symptomatic though of the struggle I had been having concerning how to corroborate my role as a pivotal protagonist concerning pedagogical tact in the data gathering. In my research I was the researcher-artist-practitioner supporting authentic expression in early childhood.

An old colleague, aware of certain aspects of my teaching history and the respect I had for process-oriented and Experiential Education approaches also came to the rescue. She suggested I return to those writings that 'spoke from the heart' and were imbued with empirical resonance of the experiences of being an artist-practitioner. Or as teacher and artist, Robin Tanner (1987) so eloquently expressed, 'being 'in harness'.

The above dilemma began to be resolved as I recommenced holding traditional company with my work journals. I began to pay closer attention to those entries leading to process writing, which concerned my felt responses to the phenomena I had observed during preliminary and pilot studies. These were situations where I was an observer without any agency in the unfolding scenes. As I found myself trying to construe a child's viewpoint and their levels of well-being and involvement, I became increasingly self aware of my own. It was the conditioned teacher-researcher reaction. I wanted to be part of the action and sharing my responses with those of other teacher-researcher colleagues. Yet, I was a student-researcher trying to examine a sometimes present, sometimes absent phenomenon that in each case made a difference to the subtle interface of child-adult interactions, and I was not involved.

4.1 The air sea rescue vignette

In a quest to regain a perspective, I returned to examine particular examples of process writing. My subsequent reflections instrumentally drew me closer to the decision to be the researcher-artist-practitioner in my data gathering in 2000. The following piece of process writing was developed post hoc from daily work journal entries made during a period of preliminary studies in the late summer and early autumn of 1999, in Brussels, Belgium. There I spent some weeks in each of the following early childhood settings: an independent, day-care, garderie/crèche and in the école maternelle/nursery classes of a state, municipal school, both in Brussels, Belgium. As I observed I also used a video camcorder and kept field notes. I referred to both when writing in my work journals. It is this extract that gave rise to the tabloid aspect of my title for this paper. As so often happens process writing may emerge out of a developing train of thought to unravel possible answers to an arising question. Such was the case concerning the air-sea rescue incident. Please note that I have made no attempt to change the style of this personal communication with its disregard at times for grammatical conventions and editing. I have only edited for reader comprehension. I commenced the entry in December 1999 by referring to the following question and response from a work journal entry of 15/09/1999:

Why are you so struck by the practice of D? (institutrice of a nursery class of 3 year olds, Schaarbeek, Brussels)

D offers an inspiring environment, and creates a scene that supports the children's own individual pace; they get the time they need to follow their train of thought processes, and actions for results.

This led to another preoccupation with reference to a work journal entry of 20/09/1999:

Why do children need to govern their own time?

As adults, a sounder way to consolidate ideas is often through a respected, uninterrupted exploration of them, which may, or may not have intervals of supportive, empathetic intervention. For the child of three years life experience there needs to be intelligent management of their environment and time spans, to encourage, support and maybe sustain their activity involvement whether the chosen activity is shared with others or not. Misplaced interruptions can cancel out thought and action processes. Well-managed interventions can enable the expansion of the child's/children's perimeter of conceptual grasp which is akin to Vygotsky's 'zone of proximal development'. Careful observation of a child's perceived train of thought and actions, intuitive in many teachers' practices, provides experienced insights into the rhythm of appropriate and supportive interventions. Likewise, the time when standing back is necessary

67

for that autonomously handled leap of conceptual grasp to take its course. Matthews (1992) says, that when this kind of child/adult inter-relationship is being perfected it is like a dance. The subtle regard of the adult upon the child's actions provides inferences for the child to utilise the adult's enlarged experience of the world. With sensitive practitioners close at hand, hopefully a child can confidently draw on adult assistance when it is needed and disregard that readily available source when they want to go it alone, stretch their boundaries of courage in what they pursue and take ownership of the results they achieve. Sharing these results with peers and adults reinforces and strengthens the methodology they have activated.

Being in command of your own learning avenues, with intelligently gauged support through access to materials, space and expertise provides a surety to one's quests and their outcomes, whether they will succeed as hoped, or not, or are a stage in a long line of repetitive and/or diverse efforts. Often the process for the imagined goal may be one of lengthy trial and error, which young children can, as a matter of consequence tackle repeatedly despite potential lack of success. Judging when to offer suggestions for achieving the goal requires the kind of practitioner's role that can read the child's intentions and understand the barriers, which may thwart, or be inhibiting success. The goal may be unobtainable, or beyond reach at a particular point of physical and mental development. The experienced practitioner can offer the means to allow the child to understand this, handle disappointment, or put the task on hold for a later attempt without the child feeling thwarted, frustrated, disabled or lacking. For both adult and child, realising, for example, that the currently presented materials are not suitable and others might be feasible when they are available may also be a level of achievement.

I linked these thoughts to an incident that I had observed in a day-care garderie/ crèche with reference to work journal entry 05/08/1999:

Two months ago, during my preliminary study in that garderie in Brussels, I watched a child of 2.5 years experiencing the process of trial and error for 15 minutes. He was persevering with a problem of weight, balance and anchorage within role-play with Duplex. He was performing an air-sea rescue accomplishment for a person whom the child had managed to heave into a dinghy and was then trying to winch up to a helicopter. He did not possess the notion of tying but understood winding. However, without the anchorage of tying the slippery string always unravelled, returning the dinghy and occupant back to its imagined stormy waters. The child provided sound effects and body sways, so it was clearly a sea of crests and troughs of considerable magnitude.

He 'fathomed' out that he had more chance if he wound the string tighter at 'sea-level' before picking up his fashioned helicopter for the winching. Without the tying element though he could not achieve his goal. He tried consistently and was not for giving up but because his efforts were not consciously recognised he was forced to when the crèche guardian on duty terminated all the children's interactions with the Duplex material. There was no flexibility. The daily routine was absolutely the issue. Without the tact of informed pedagogical awareness there was no subtle intervention to support his intense involvement and its zone of proximal development. It was not noted that here was a child on the brink of conceptual extension. No discussion occurred about how to make provision for him to return to the problem solving issue he was involved with at another time or juncture. This is not to deny that the same problem with its conceptual strivings will not arise or be encountered again in many other situations later. It is not that there is no point of return, perhaps via another parallel experience. Nonetheless, it is too frequently and intolerably frustrating to be the 'fly on the wall' and unable to be involved in another capacity to encourage, by 'tips' or 'hints' whilst the involvement of a child has achieved such profundity.

I tried to unpack the personal impact of this episode further. It was far from being an isolated observation where children's activities seem invisible to those in loco parentis. It encapsulated for me the value of teachers as daily researchers using for example, the instruments of the Experiential Education programme (EXE) developed by Laevers et al (1994b, 1997a, 1997b); also used in the Effective Early Learning programme (EEL), (Pascal, 1993; Pascal et al, (1994, 1998). It also kept me centred on solving how; in my research methodology and methods I could practically parallel this paradigm as a university based student-researcher:

The crèche workers in the garderie loved the children. They consistently expressed warmth and care for the physical security of their charges but their level of training and/or further professional development depleted their pedagogic understanding of cognitive development. Those in the partnership of caring for and educating young children need appropriate and meaningful training. It also needs the development of unconditional self-awareness that use of the Leuven Adult Observation Scale in Early Childhood Education. (ASOS-ECE) through training encourages. Awareness and understanding of those myriad trains of thought and action in conceptual gatherings of children requires an entirely different attitude in the minds and actions of practitioners. Self-awareness and evaluation of one's own conceptual gathering expeditions and their outcomes seems to be a prerequisite. Listening to, observing finitely, and feeling the rhythm of paths for cognition provides insightful means for

69

learning environment opportunities and their provision. Likewise, gauged, meaningful interventions through an understanding of the practitioner's own parallel, more developed levels of conceptual gathering journeys. Being in tune thus opens up and harnesses communication channels to support the travels of those younger minds towards being on the edge of their perimeters of cognition and making that leap for personal triumph.
(14, 15/12/1999)

4.2 Work journals as part of data gathering

My self-awareness of the 'lived experience' of involvement by adult and child protagonists seemed to be a key to research an adult-child interface phenomenon that may facilitate authentic expression in a particular sense for 'visual describing' as well as holistically. The voice of certainty was reasserted, and in April, May and June 2000, I carried out my main research site data gathering in a nursery school. There I worked as researcher-artist-practitioner with small groups of 3-5 year olds. The chosen children were the 'leavers' who in September would commence primary education. They were involved in acts of 'visual describing': expressively constructing meaning vocally, graphically, and through modelling. Thus an empirical realm was the starting point for my research journey to seek an understanding of the phenomenon of a pedagogic way of being.

I also decided to use work journals to form part of the research data. This changed their very private status when for research purposes the often very personal shorthand, as in my field notebooks, has to be transcribed and committed to be openly accountable, intelligible and accessible.

4.3 Finding the term for the research phenomenon

Later I found a more quintessential term when, sensitively aware of the paradigm I was seeking, my current adviser, Dr Peter John introduced me to the work of phenomenologist, Max van Manen. Peter John is not only an historian, deeply interested in the power and potential fidelity of narrative but also a teacher with a commitment to school-based teacher-research. Part of his work is enquiry into concepts concerning the intuitive practitioner (John, 2000). Furthermore he is a painter, novelist and parent. To have overlapping areas of interest can be potentially fruitful but above all is the possible strengthening of autonomy through confidently sensing that one's viewpoint is being considered empathetically. I pursued the references and was arrested by van Manen's term 'pedagogical tact' (1990, 1991); it satisfied my notion of the phenomenon I was trying describe.

4.4 Using work journals for process writing about literature searches

The following is an example of 'process writing' from compilations of work journal entries in 2001, exploring the role I had decided upon for my main research site data collection and aspects of the supportive literature:

The overall regard for, and experience of the data is the 'lived experience' of human science research (Van Manen, 1984-2001).

Running through the theoretical and practical aspects of my research study as with this entry is an awareness of its 'lived experience' being fundamental to its construction; its raison d'être. 'Lived experience' explains the needful reason for, and position of a researcher-artist-practitioner's role in my research and is informed by certain teacher-researcher and researcher-teacher perspectives and methodologies. Regarding the teacher-researcher position whereby research is seen as being fundamental to praxis I have looked specifically to Stenhouse (1980, 1988, and in Hopkins and Ruddick, 1985) and Malaguzzi and the Reggio philosophy (Edwards et al, 1998; Dahlberg et al, 1999). The emphasis is shifted subtlety concerning the researcher-teacher perspective. In the case of my study, a university-based researcher whose early childhood practices as an educator are a focus for 'early childhood setting' research, this is a perspective examined by Duckworth (1991), Paley (1990) and Britsch (1995). Here the difference is a compilation of both the above positions, whereby, in terms of the nature of data gathering and my particular involvement it has to be explained why I am the researcher-artist-practitioner. By undertaking research as a university-based student-researcher with a developing social science research perspective, I wanted to build on the activity of teacher-researcher. The kind of activity I had been familiar with during most of my teaching career but with an opportunity for the theoretical focus to be managed within a different time element. Britsch (1995) says that her own doctoral research (1992) took this path of theoretical and practical interplay between the positions of teacher and researcher. She describes this meld of roles as having a Janus-faced nature where 'the researcher draws on teacher skills, and the teacher draws on the research perspective and continuously walks the line between the moment-to-moment demands of each role,' thereby constructing and defining an 'enactment-of-self in the classroom.' (1995, p. 297).

4.5 Discussion of some theoretical perspectives

I conclude with a brief summary of some theoretical perspectives informing my ongoing research inquiries regarding pedagogical tact and the support of authentic expression in early childhood.

According to Matthews (1999a; 1999b) children construct meaning through their authentic expression. The routes for their construction of meaning may embrace, for example, the employment, of paint, drawing implements, modelling materials and tools, as well as juxtapositional interfusions of motion and vocalisation. I use the term, 'acts of visual describing' to encompass the breadth of these exploratory and expressive processes. The depth of children's authentic expression during visual describing episodes may be enhanced or hindered by the quality of interaction between adult and child (Anning, 1999; Matthews, 1992,1999a; 1999b). Anning (1999) noted, that where practitioners converge with children who have completed an act of visual describing, or are still in the process it is rare for the adult party to realise it as a communicative act, where there is reciprocity, and a serious dialogue of recognition takes place. As Laevers (2000) has found, the personality of a teacher having an experiential teacher style may exert a powerful and beneficial influence upon the adult-child dynamic. He states that the teacher's sensitivity is evidenced in responses, which demonstrate empathetic understanding of the basic emotional, physical and cognitive needs of the child. A practitioner's 'pedagogical tact' (Van Manen, 1990, 1991; 1995) is a phenomenological conveyance that intuitively perceives the child's need for attention, affirmation, security, affection and clarity of the means to proceed, and responds appropriately. For the present, I have to understand tact as the governor of, and pedagogical concern for an informed, altruistic way of being with young children in the immediate of their experiences in an early childhood setting.

The human science approach for this research is phenomenological. It is seeking meaning through interpretative writing of an experiential process. This involves immersions in the traditions of phenomenology in a scholarly way, and through validating engagement in overlapping circles of inquiry that can never be absolute although it can be accepted that a shared recognition may draw us toward it.

5 Conclusion

Maintaining faith with concepts that have been acknowledged intuitively but then need to be shared through informed articulated expression is a difficult process. Confidence in the sometimes, raw committed writings and sketched images of my work journals has helped to restore that development. Leonardo da Vinci spoke of his 'Notebooks' (Mc Curdy, 1906) as places to secrete the universal aspects of perceptual self-illustration developing from early beginnings and throughout life. I hope I may continue to practise this method and learn from both the process and the product.

References

Anning, A. (1999). Learning to draw and drawing to learn. *Journal of Art and Education, 18*, 163-172.

Britsch, S. J. (1992). The development "story" within the culture of the preschool (Doctoral dissertation, University of California, Berkeley). *Dissertation Abstracts International, 54*, 2045A-2046A.

Britsch, S. J. (1995). The researcher as teacher: Constructing one's place in the story of events of preschoolers. *International Journal of Qualitative Studies in Education, 8*, 297-309.

Dahlberg, G., Moss, P., & Pence, A. (1999). *Beyond quality in early childhood education and care: Postmodern perspectives.* London: Routledge Falmer.

Duckworth, E. (1991). Twenty-four, forty-two and I love you: Keeping it complex. *Harvard Review. 61*, 1-24.

Edwards, C., Gandini, L., & Forman, G. (Eds.) (1998). *The hundred languages of children: The Reggio Emilia approach - advanced reflections.* London: Ablex.

Eisner, E. W. (1979). The contribution of painting to children's cognitive development. *Journal of Curriculum Studies, 11*, 109-116.

Gendlin, E.T. (1964). A theory of personality change. In P. Worchel & D. Byrne, D (Eds.), *Personality change.* New York: Wiley.

Heiddegger, M. (1962). *Being and time.* New York: Harper and Row.

John, P. (2000). Awareness and intuition: How student teachers read their own lessons. In T. Atkinson & G. Claxton (Eds.), *The intuitive practitioner.* Buckingham: Open University Press.

Jones, L. (2001). Trying to break bad habits in practice by engaging with poststructuralist theories. *Early Years: An International Journal of Research and Development, 21*, 25-32.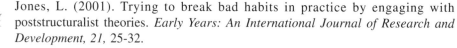

Laevers, F. (1993). Deep-level-learning as an exemplary application in the area of physical knowledge. *European Early Childhood Education Research Journal, 1*, 53-68.

Laevers, F. (1994a). The innovative project "Experiential Education" and the definition of quality in education. In F. Laevers (Ed.), *Defining and assessing quality in early childhood education.* Leuven: Leuven University Press.

Laevers, F., (Ed.) (1994b). *The Leuven Involvement Scale for Young Children* [manual and videotape]. Leuven: Centre for Experiential Education.

Laevers, F., Bogaerts, M., & Moons, J. (1997a). *Experiential Education at Work. A Setting with 5-Year Olds* [manual and videotape]. Leuven: Centre for Experiential Education.

Laevers, F., Vandenbussche, E., Kog, M., & Moons, J. (1997b). *A Process-Oriented Child Monitoring Scale for Young Children.* Leuven: Centre for Experiential Education.

Laevers, F. (1998). Understanding the world of objects and people: Intuition as a core element of deep-level-learning. *International Journal of Educational Research, 29,* 25-38.

Laevers, F. (2000). Forward to basics! Deep-level-learning and the experiential approach. *Early Years: An International Journal of Research and Development, 20* (2), 20-29.

Mason, J. (1996). *Personal enquiry: Moving from concern towards research.* Milton Keynes: Open University Press.

Matthews, J. (1992). The genesis of aesthetic sensibility. In D. Thistlewood, S. Paine & E. Court (Eds.). *Drawing research and development* (pp. 26-39). Harlow: Longman Group UK Limited.

Matthews, J. (1999a). *The art of childhood and adolescence: The construction of meaning.* London: Falmer Press.

Matthews, J. (1999b). Why children are drawing such attention. *Early Years Educaton,1* (2), 22-26.

Mc Curdy, E. (1938). *Leonardo da Vinci's Note-Books.* London, (New edition in 2 vols; arranged, rendered into English and introduced bij E. Mc Curdy). London: Jonathan Cape.

Paley, V. G. (1990). *The boy who would be a helicopter: The uses of storytelling in the classroom.* Cambridge: Harvard University Press.

Pascal, C. (1993). Capturing the quality of educational provision for young children: A story of developing professionals and developing methodology. *European Early Childhood Education Research Journal, 1,* 69-80.

Pascal, C., Bertram, A., & Ramsden, F. (1994). *Effective Early Learning Project: The quality evaluation and development process.* Worcester: Amber Publishing.

Pascal, C., Bertram, T., Mould, C., & Hall, R. (1998). Exploring the relationship between process and outcome in young children's learning: Stage one of a longitudinal study. *International Journal of Educational Research, 29*, 51-67.

Rinaldi, C. (1998). Projected curriculum constructed through documentation - Progettazione: An interview with Lella Gandini. In C. Edwards L. Gandini & G. Forman (Eds.), *The hundred languages of children: The Reggio Emilia approach - advanced reflections*. Greenwich: Ablex Pub. Corp.

Ruddick, J. & Hopkins, D. (1985). *Research as a basis for teaching: Readings from the work of Lawrence Stenhouse*. London: Heinemann Educatonal Books.

Stenhouse, L. (1980). The study of samples and the study of cases. *British Educational Research Journal, 6*, 1-6.

Stenhouse, L. (1988). Case study methods. In J. P. Keeves (Ed.), *Educational research, methodology and measurement: An international handbook* (2nd ed.) (pp. 49 – 53). Oxford: Pergamon.

Tanner, R. (1987). *Double harness: An autobiography*. London: Impact Books.

Tolkien, J. R. R. (1954/55). *The Lord of the rings*: *The fellowship of the ring; The twin towers*; *The return of the king*. Great Britain: George Allen & Unwin.

Van Manen, M. (1984). Practicing phenomenological writing. *Phenomenolgy & Pedagogy, 2*, 36-69.

Van Manen, M. (1990). *Researching lived experience: Human science for an action sensitive pedagogy*. London: The Althouse Press.

Van Manen, M. (1991). *The tact of teaching: The meaning of pedagogical thoughtfulness*. London: The Althouse Press.

Van Manen, M. (1994). Pedagogy, virtue, and narrative identity in teaching. *Curriculum Inquiry, 4*(2). Retrieved April 25, 2001, from: http://www.ualberta.ca/-vanmanen/virtue.htm

Van Manen, M. (1995). On the epistemology of reflective practice. *Teachers and Teaching: Theory and Practice, 1*(1). Retrieved July 26, 2001, from: http://www.ualberta.ca/-vanmanen/epistpractice.htm

Van Manen, M. (1996). Phenomenological pedagogy and the question of meaning. In Vandenburg (Ed.). *Phenomenology and educational discourse* (pp. 39 – 64). Durban: Heinemann Higher and Further Education.

Van Manen, M. (1999). The practice of practice. In M. Lange, J. Olsen, W. Henning & W. Bunder (Eds.). *Changing schools/changing practices: perspectives on educational reform and teacher professionalism.* Leuven: Garant.

Van Manen, M. (2000). Moral language and pedagogical experience. *The Journal of Curriculum Studies, 32* (2). Retrieved Juin 15, 2001, from: http://www.ualberta.ca/-vanmanen/moral_language.htm

Van Manen, M. (2001). Phenomenology online. http://www.atl.ualberta.ca/po/inquiry

Vecchi, V. (1998). The Role of the atelierista: An interview with Lella Gandini. In C. Edwards, L. Gandini & G. Forman (Eds.). *The hundred languages of children: The Reggio Emilia approach – advanced reflections.* Greenwich: Ablex Pub. Corp.

The Effective Early Learning Project:
The quality of adult engagement in early childhood settings in the UK

Christine Pascal, Tony Bertram

1 Introduction

This paper provides emerging evidence on the quality of 'adult engagement' experienced by three and four year old children in a range of early education and care settings in the UK. The evidence was gathered and analyzed from observations undertaken as part of the Effective Early Learning (EEL) Project. An assessment of the quality of adult educative interactions forms a central part of the EEL Project evaluative methodology. This key process variable in children's learning is viewed as critical in determine the effectiveness of educational provision and in informing the improvement process in early childhood settings. As such, the results of the adult practitioner observations provide illuminative evidence of the quality of young children's learning experiences. These findings have a particular relevance given the current debate about the quality of teaching and learning in early childhood settings in the UK. It also provides interesting data for a comparative analysis of the UK results and those in Portugal and The Netherlands.

2 What is the Effective Early Learning project?

The EEL Project (Pascal & Bertram, 1997), is an international research and development initiative which aims to evaluate and improve the quality of early learning in a wide range of education and care settings throughout the UK, The Netherlands and Portugal (Pascal et al. 1997, 1998). The work of the Project has been largely funded by a partnership between The Esmee Fairbairn Charitable Trust, University College Worcester and local authority providers of education and care. The Project is now in its fifth year of operation.

The EEL Project arose out of the growing recognition that the early years of a child's life are the most critical learning years and will have a long term effect on subsequent achievement and progress (Sylva & Wiltshire, 1993; Ball, 1994; Schweinhart & Weikart, 1997). It also followed the growing awareness that many education and care contexts were not providing the quality early learning experiences that research has shown are essential to long term success (Audit Commission 1996, OFSTED, 1998). The inadequacy of early learning experiences for many groups of young children growing up across the UK was felt to be a major contributor to their later lack of achievement within the school system and beyond (Ball, 1994). The Project therefore aimed to develop a cost effective and efficient strategy for enhancing the quality of early learning experiences for young children in education and care settings from the private, voluntary and public sectors.

The Effective Early Learning Research Project began work in May 1993 and grew out of the urgent need for procedures to facilitate quality evaluation and improvement in the diverse range of settings in which under fives are being educated in the UK. It also responded to the lack of a substantial empirical data base on the quality and effectiveness of early learning offered in these settings. In its early stages the research focused particularly on provision for 3 and 4 year olds, as these children are currently in a wider range of provision than any other age group, but its methods and principles are applicable to teaching and learning at any age. The Project is operating throughout the UK and is being carried out by a team of practitioner researchers, directed by Professor Christine Pascal and Dr Tony Bertram, based at the Centre for Research in Early Childhood at Worcester College of Higher Education in the UK.

The key aims of the Project are:

1. To develop a cost-effective strategy to evaluate and improve the quality and effectiveness of early learning available to young children in a wide range of education and care settings across England, Wales, Scotland and Northern Ireland.

2. To evaluate and compare rigorously and systematically the quality of early learning provided in the diverse range of early childhood education and care settings which characterise provision in the UK.

The project centres round the development and application of an innovative, cost effective and manageable set of 'Quality Evaluation and Improvement' procedures which may be used for training, institutional development, monitoring and review in all early childhood settings. The development of quantitative and qualitative instruments to evaluate and compare the quality of provision in different settings is also a key feature of the Project. In short, it has developed, trialled extensively, and disseminated, a manageable and practicable system of 'externally validated participant researchers in their own settings. This ensures that the knowledge generated by the Project has a powerful and direct application to the realities of life in these early childhood settings.

3 Who is involved in the EEL project?

The Project has at its heart two interlinked, and complementary elements; that of research and development. A main thrust of the Project's work is to develop and improve the quality and effectiveness of young children's learning. This operates through the implementation of a process of externally validated self-evaluation, which leads directly to action planning and improvement. This process of evaluation is providing a wealth of detailed qualitative and quantitative data from early childhood settings across the UK. Data on such things as training, staff ratios, curriculum, facilities, teaching styles, interactions, daily programmes, planning and assessment procedures, equal opportunities, home/school partnership and quality control procedures have been collected. This allows a comparative assessment to be made of different kinds of provision, and has also validated a set of research instruments and methods for quality monitoring and review of early childhood services. It is anticipated that the research analysis will be published later on this year.

The links between the research process and practice are clear in this Project. The Project is grounded in practice; the research being informed by, and informing, practitioners. The roles of researcher and practitioner have become interwoven in the process. All the members of the research team are practitioners by training and are able to take on this role within the settings they work. This gives them credibility within the settings and helps to break down some of the distancing and mystique, which sometimes surrounds "research". Practitioners too have become participant researchers in their own settings. This ensures that the knowledge generated by the Project has a powerful and direst application to the realities of life in these early childhood settings.

The Project provides a clear and targeted strategy for change and improvement which builds upon the existing range of provision for young children and attempts to extend the skills and expertise of all those who work with young children. It brings together education and care.

Phase 1, from 1993-1994, was a 'Developmental' period, during which members of the EEL Team worked intensively for twelve months in 13 different education and care settings, with 52 practitioners and 390 children and families. The aim was to work in partnership with and parents to create a manageable system of quality evaluation and improvement.

Phase 2, from 1994-1995, was a period of 'Consolidation and Data Gathering', during which the EEL procedures were trialled and data gathered in 200+ different education and care settings from 9 local authorities, by 800+ practitioners, and 6,000+ children and families.

The aim was to train practitioners within each of the participating settings, to work with external advisers, who would support them through the EEL process of 'Quality Evaluation and Improvement'. Data for the national research element of the Project was also collected by the trained practitioners, and validated by the external advisers.

Phase 3, from 1995-1996, was a period of 'Dissemination and Data Gathering', during which the EEL procedures were further disseminated to 500+ different education and care settings from 22 local authorities, by 2,300 practitioners and 15,000+ children and families. The aim was to continue a national training programme for practitioners from participating settings, to work with a developing group of trained external advisers, to implement the EEL 'Quality Evaluation and Improvement' process across the UK. Data was also gathered by this larger cohort to complete the evidential base for the Project research strategy.

Phase 4, from 1996 on, set in motion an ongoing period of 'Dissemination and Data Analysis", during which the EEL 'Quality Evaluation and Improvement' procedures will be widely disseminated throughout the UK and beyond, through a national programme of accredited training. Currently over 50 local authorities are committed to this programme. Data from Phases 2, 3 and 4 are undergoing analysis to provide a detailed and comprehensive portrait of the quality of early learning provision for 3 and 4 year olds in the UK, and it is data from these Phases that are reported in this paper.

The whole life of the EEL project has been and continues to be, developmental and collaborative. From the onset, we worked in partnership with practitioners, and during the last five years this partnership has grown and evolved, with each of the partners extending their role in the process. In particular, the practitioners in later phases of the Project have taken over responsibility for most of the evaluation and improvement process, benefiting from the support and validation of an eel external advisor at key points, this 'groundedness' provides the eel procedures with validity, credibility and strength. The experience of the last four years have shown that 'Quality Evaluation and Improvement' is a process well within the grasp of all those who work with young children. Those we have worked with have embraced the rigorous and critical procedures with professionalism and dedication, and an overriding commitment to improving the quality of their work with young children.

4 Evaluation methodology

4.1 The Evaluation and improvement process

Building on the principles of action, quality is evaluated using the EEL framework by taking the participants through a systematic and rigorous four stage process of 'Evaluation and Improvement'.

Stage 1: Evaluation – during which researchers and participants work together to document and evaluate the quality of early learning within the setting.

Stage2: Action Planning – during which researchers and participants meet together to identify priorities for action and to generate an action plan to implement this.

Stage 3: Improvement – during which the action plan to improve the quality of provision is implemented.

Stage 4: Reflection – during which participants are encouraged to reflect upon the Evaluation and Development process and to review the impact of the action plan in the light of experience.

4.2 The Evaluation stage

In the first phase of Evaluation, the team of practitioners within the setting work together with an eel external advisor, parents and children to scrutinise the quality of their provision. The quality of practice in relation to 10 dimensions of quality are carefully documented and evaluated using a number of research methods in which the Project participants are trained. These include detailed observations of children and adults, interviews of parents, colleagues and children, documentary analysis and a number of questionnaires. One if the key and innovatory features of this project is that it allows a detailed, rigorous quantitative and qualitative assessment to be made of the quality of educational provision across a wide range of different early childhood settings. This process of quality assessment has been enhanced by the utilisation of two key observation techniques, which measure the effectiveness of the learning and teaching process. These two methods are:

- the Child Involvement Scale: or Leuven Involvement Scale for Young Children LIS-YC (Laevers 1996), which measures the level of involvement (deep-level-learning) of the children in the activities offered

- the Adult Engagement Scale (ASOS) which measures the qualities of effective teaching demonstrated by the adult

The social psychological underpinning of these techniques and their methodology are detailed by Laevers (1996) and Pascal and Bertram (1997). A short summary of the content and the way we have used the Adult Engagement Scale is outlined below.

The Adult Engagement Scale (Laevers 1994, Bertram 1996, Pascal et al. 1998) provides a central part of the quality assessment process. This instrument is also based on a method developed by Laevers' EXE project called the Adult Style Observation Schedule (ASOS), but we have modified it for use in the EEL Project. This evaluative instrument provides an assessment measure quality of an adult's interactions with a child. The instrument is based on the notion that he style of interactions between the educator and the child is a critical factor in the effectiveness of the learning experience. The instrument identifies three core elements in a teacher's style, which shapes the quality of such interactions:

SENSITIVITY: This is the sensitivity of the adult to the feelings and emotional well being of the child and includes elements of sincerity, empathy, responsiveness and affection.

STIMULATION: This is the way in which the adult intervenes in a learning process and the content of such interventions.

AUTONOMY: This is the degree of freedom, which the adult gives the child to experiment, make judgements, and choose activities and express ideas. It also includes how the adult handles conflict, rules and behavioural issues.

These two quantitative research methods provide hard data of the effect of action on the quality of educative interaction (teaching) in each setting, as scores obtained in the Evaluation stage can be compared with scores following the Improvement stage. Interestingly, although we term this data as "Quantitative" the scale is an attempt to measure "qualitative" aspects of the teaching and learning process. The results reported in this paper are based on data gained using the Adult Engagement Scale assessments.

5 Research sample

The Adult Engagement observations were conducted in nine different types of early childhood education and education settings drawn from 23 local authorities throughout the UK. These settings included:

Table 1: Research sample

PRIVATE SECTOR	
Private Day Nurseries	11
Workplace Nurseries	23
VOLUNTARY SECTOR	
PLA Pre-Schools (Playgroups)	42
STATE SECTOR	
Primary School Reception Classes	91
Primary School Nursery Classes	77
Nursery Schools	33
Primary School Early Years Units	13
Family Centres	16
Special Schools	17
TOTAL	**323**

These settings were self selecting settings that had opted into the EEL Project and the staff had all been trained in the EEL evaluation methodologies, including the Adult Engagement Scale. Practitioners within the settings conducted the observations in two rounds, one before the EEL improvement process (15,170 observations) and one after (11,340 observations). These observations were validated internally by the study practitioners, and then externally by an EEL External Advisor. In addition, a sample of settings (approx. 10%) were visited by EEL researchers to out a validity check on the reported data.

The settings included in the sample covered the private, voluntary and state funded sectors. It should be noted that our analysis of the EEL contextual data gathered at the same time as these observations reveals the State Sector settings generally have a higher level of qualified staff working within them, including trained graduate teachers. The level of resourcing, facilities and equipment available is also generally better in the State Sector, and very variable within the Voluntary Sector settings. The adult-child ratios were also very variable across sectors, with the Private and Voluntary Sectors generally having lower ratios than the State Sector, except in Special Schools.

6 Results of adult engagement assessments

The Adult Engagement data are represented in four parts:

1. Means between Three Engagement Domains
2. Sensitivity Levels
3. Stimulation Levels
4. Autonomy Levels

6.1 Means between three engagement domains

The adult observational data recorded the levels of Sensitivity, Stimulation and Autonomy displayed by practitioners in their educative interactions with children. A score from 1 to 5 was recorded for each of the three domains in each observation in all settings. When we compare the results from the three domains, taking all settings scores as a whole, we can see a clear hierarchical pattern. Settings in all cases consistently displayed high levels in relation to Sensitivity and the lowest levels in Autonomy. This pattern confirms the hierarchical, developmental pattern of adult interactive skills identified by Bertram (1996) within the UK educational and care provision.

Table 2: Engagement means

Engagement Domain	Round 1	Round 2
Sensitivity	4.37	4.51
Stimulation	3.54	3.79
Autonomy	2.78	3.12

These data demonstrate that:

- sensitivity to children is a basic precondition for educative interactions to take place

- stimulation occurs once a level of sensitivity and responsiveness between adults and children has been established

- autonomy is the most challenging aspect of effective educative interactions, and might be viewed as a higher order educative skill

6.2 Sensitivity levels

Table 3: Sensitivity data

Type of Setting	Round 1	Round 2
Private Day Nursery	4.33	4.60
Workplace Nursery	4.19	4.38
PLA Pre-School	4.03	4.37
Reception Class	4.39	4.42
Nursery Class	4.42	4.52
Nursery School	4.54	4.65
Early Years Unit	4.42	4.48
Family Centre	4.27	4.36
Special School	4.71	4.81

Figure 1: Mean sensitivity of each type of setting

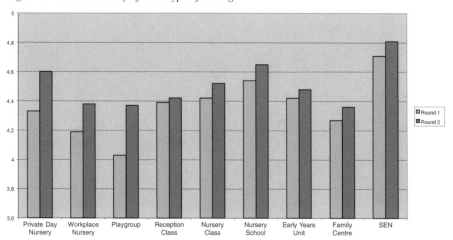

Data shown in Table 3 and Figure 1 reveal that the mean level of Sensitivity for the settings as a whole is 4.37 in the first round and 4.51 in the second round. These reveal a high level of Sensitivity displayed in adult educative interactions in all study settings. They also show that all settings increased their sensitivity level following the implementation of the EEL improvement process.

When we compare sensitivity levels between different types of setting we can see that the Special Schools demonstrate the highest levels (4.19/4.81), followed by the Nursery Schools (4.54/4.65). the lowest levels of Sensitivity are found in PLA Pre-Schools (4.03/4.37), followed by Workplace Nurseries (4.19/4.38). When we compare Sensitivity mean scores for different sectors we see that the State Sector demonstrates the highest levels (4.46/4.54) and the Voluntary Sector has the lowest levels (4.03/4.37)

These data demonstrate that:

- practitioners in all settings demonstrate high levels of Sensitivity in their educative interactions with children

- sensitivity levels are highest in the State sector and lowest in the Voluntary Sector

- that the EEL evaluation and improvement process increased the Sensitivity levels of practitioners

- sensitivity levels are highest in Special Schools and Nursery Schools, and lowest in PLA Pre-Schools

6.3 Stimulation levels

Table 4: Stimulation data

Type of Setting	Round 1	Round 2
Private Day Nursery	3.46	3.91
Workplace Nursery	3.41	3.54
PLA Pre-School	3.27	3.70
Reception Class	3.61	3.72
Nursery Class	3.68	3.76
Nursery School	3.71	3.92
Early Years Unit	3.37	3.76
Family Centre	3.47	3.66
Special School	3.88	4.14

Data shown in Table 4 and Figure 2 reveal that the mean level of Stimulation for the settings as a whole is 3.54 in the first round and 3.79 in the second round. These data reveal overall a fairly good level of Stimulation displayed in adult educative interactions in most study settings, although the levels are

Figure 2: Mean stimulation of each type of setting

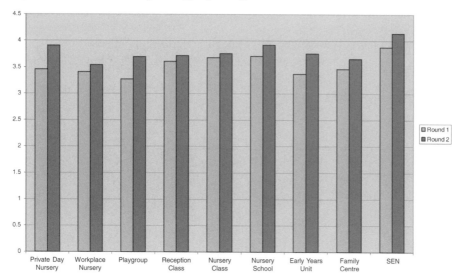

significantly variable between settings. They also show that all settings increased their Stimulation level following the implementation of the EEL improvement process.

When we compare Stimulation levels between different types of setting we can see that the Special Schools demonstrate the highest levels of Stimulation (3.88/4.14), followed by the Nursery Schools (3.71/3.92). the lowest levels of Stimulation are found in PLA Pre-Schools in the first round of observations (3.27/3.70), followed by the Workplace Nurseries 3.41), but by the second round of observations the PLA Pre-Schools (3.70) were higher than the Workplace Nurseries (3.54) and the Family Centres (3.66).

When we compare Stimulation mean scores for different Sectors we see that the State Sector demonstrates the highest levels (3.62/3.83) and the Voluntary Sector has the lowest levels (3.27/3.70)

The data demonstrates that:

- stimulation levels are variable across different types of setting, with some settings displaying very high levels and others significantly lower

- the EEL evaluation and improvement process increased the Stimulation levels of practitioners, and had a particular impact in the Voluntary Sector settings

- stimulation levels are highest in the State Sector and Lowest in the Voluntary Sector

- stimulation levels are highest in Special Schools and Nursery Schools, and lowest in Workplace Nurseries, Family Centres and PLA Pre-Schools

6.4 Autonomy levels

Table 5: Autonomy data

Type of Setting	Round 1	Round 2
Private Day Nursery	2.87	3.37
Workplace Nursery	2.64	2.94
PLA Pre-School	2.69	3.11
Reception Class	2.65	2.90
Nursery Class	2.90	3.22
Nursery School	2.96	3.21
Early Years Unit	2.51	3.20
Family Centre	2.71	3.11
Special School	3.05	3.08

Figure 3: Mean autonomy of each type of setting

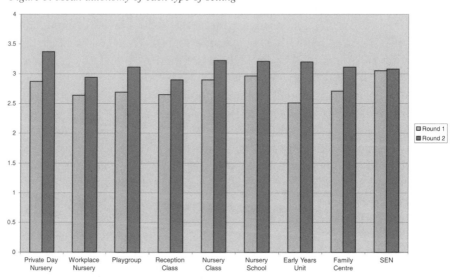

Data shown in Table 5 and Figure 3 reveal that the mean level of Autonomy for the settings as a whole is 2.78 in the first round and 3.12 in the second round. These reveal a relatively low level of autonomy displayed in adult educative interactions in all study settings. They also show that all settings increased their Autonomy level following the implementation of the EEL improvement process.

When we compare Autonomy levels between different types of setting we can see that in the first round of observations the Special Schools demonstrate the highest level (3.05), followed by the Nursery Schools (2.96) and the Nursery Classes (2.90). the lowest levels of Autonomy in the first round are found in the Early Years Units (2.51), followed by the Workplace Nurseries (2.64) and the Reception Classes (2.65). interestingly, in the second round of observations of Autonomy the highest levels are to be found in the Private Day Nurseries (3.37), the Nursery Classes (3.22) and the Nursery Schools (3.21). The lowest levels continue to be found in the Reception Classes (2.90) and Workplace Nurseries (2.94).

When we compare Autonomy mean scores for different sectors we see that the State Sector demonstrates the highest levels (2.80) in the first round but the Private Sector had the highest in the second round (3.16). The lowest levels of Autonomy are found in the Voluntary Sector in both rounds (2.69/3.11), but the State Sector displayed almost equally low levels in the second round (3.12).

This data demonstrates that:

- practitioners in all settings demonstrate relatively low levels of Autonomy in their educative interactions with children

- the EEL evaluation and improvement process increased the Autonomy levels of practitioners

- autonomy levels are consistently higher in Nursery schools and Classes and consistently lower in Reception Classes and Workplace Nurseries

- autonomy levels are consistently lower in the Voluntary Sector than the State Sector or the Private Sector

7 Discussion

These results provide an illuminative portrait of the quality of 'Adult Engagement' in early years settings within the UK. They indicate that the quality of educative interactions is variable within and between sectors of provision. There are a number of key findings, which are summarised below:

- there is a hierarchical relationship between the three domains of Sensitivity, Stimulation and Autonomy in educative interactions in all settings, with Sensitivity being consistently high and Autonomy being consistently low

- practitioners in all settings display high Sensitivity in their educative interactions with young children

- the levels of Stimulation are generally higher in the State Sector settings, where more highly qualified staff are employed, particularly in those settings where a trained teacher is employed

- the levels of Autonomy are low in all Sectors and settings, but are particularly low in PLA Pre-Schools and Primary School Reception Classes

- overall, the Voluntary Sector settings score consistently lower on all domains of 'adult engagement', while the State Sector score higher on all domains

- all settings respond to training and those settings with less qualified staff make the greatest progress

The above results present an interesting portrait of the pattern of adult educative interactions in UK early childhood settings. The key role of training, particularly of teacher training, is indicated in ensuring children are appropriately stimulated in these interactions. The factors inhibiting Autonomy in these interactions, particularly with Primary School Reception Classes and PLA Pre-Schools will be further explored in the analysis of the EEL contextual data. Assessment of the quality of adult educative interactions in Private, Voluntary and State Sector settings demonstrate that better quality is generally found in State Sector settings.

References

Audit Commission (1996). *Counting to five.* London: Author.

Ball, C. (1994). *Start Right: The importance of early learning.* London: RSA.

Bertram A.D.(1996). *Effective educators of young children: Developing a methodology for improvement.* Doctoral dissertation, Coventry University.

Laevers F. (1994). *The Leuven Involvement Scale for Young Children* [manual and videotape]. Leuven: Centre for Experiential Education.

Laevers F. (Ed.) (1996). *An exploration of the concept of involvement as an indicator for quality in early childhood education.* Dundee: Scottish Consultative Council on the Curriculum.

Office For Standards in Education (OFSTED) (1998). *The quality of education in institutions inspected under the nursery education funding arrangements.* London: Author.

Pascal, C. & Bertram, A.D. (Eds.) (1997). *Effective early learning: Case studies in improvement.* London: Hodder and Stoughton.

Pascal, C., Bertram, A.D., Ramsden F., Georgeson J., Saunders M. & Mould C. (1998). *Evaluating and developing quality in early childhood settings: A professional development programme.* Worcester: Amber Publications.

Schweinhart, L.J. & Weikart, D.P. (1997). *Lasting differences: The High/Scope Preschool Curriculum Comparison.* USA: High/Scope Educational Research Foundation, High/Scope Press.

Sylva, K. & Wiltshire, J. (1993). The impact of early learning on children's later development. *European Early Childhood Education Research Journal, 1*, 17-41.

THE ADULT ROLE
IN FINNISH EARLY CHILDHOOD EDUCATION AND CARE
Marjatta Kalliala, Leena Tahkokallio

1 Part 1

1.1 Background

When we discuss the current adult role in Finnish early childhood education, it is essential to understand what is characteristic of ECEC (early childhood education and care) in Finland. It is also necessary to describe what the most fundamental changes have been during the past two decades, and to be conscious of the two levels of change. When new concepts occur in speech and new ways of thinking seem to be widely accepted, it does not mean that there are changes in the practice that could be interpreted as the expected outcome of these new ways of looking at children and their learning. How does the constructivist way of learning or child-initiated pedagogy change the practice and daily routines in Finnish day-care centres? How do the changes in the discourse influence the adult role? It is not at all obvious that there is a logical connection between talk and practice. On the contrary, the discourse sometimes seems to live its own life far removed from life at the day-care centres. Thus, in trying to grasp the Finnish reality, it is necessary to look at the official ECEC policy as well as beyond it.

The unconditional right to day care. The Act on Children's Day Care came into force in 1973 and, with further additions, paved the way for the accepted Finnish position that every child has the right to day care. Every child under school age has the unconditional right to day care provided by the local authority once the mother's or father's period of parental allowance comes to an end, irrespective of the parents' financial status or whether they are working (Ministry of Social Affairs and Health, 2000).

Day care was previously seen as a social service for parents who were working or studying. It was also based on social factors. The unconditional right to day care was meant to emphasise the child's right to ECE and the parents' right to decide when this right should be used (Karila & Nummenmaa, 2001, p. 14). In reality, it means that parents have the unconditional right to put their child into full-time care after the maternity leave at the age of one or even less.

Educare. The Finnish describe their system of early care and education as 'educare', seeing it as a system which carefully blends care and education and where play is understood as the central tool of both teaching and learning (Karila & Nummenmaa 2001, p. 11-14; OECD, 2001, p. 21). It is easy to agree with this approach. The well being of the child demands a holistic view; it is not possible to leave care or education aside if we want to satisfy the child's needs in the best way. However, the educare approach also means a tension between the two objectives and it is not always easy to find the ideal balance between them. Thus the educare approach constantly raises questions like how the staff members should be trained, whether everybody on the staff should be expert in care and education, who is responsible for teaching, how much emphasis should be put on care routines and how much on pedagogy? As to the trendy multi-professional teams - should the division of labour be based on professional education or on the ideology of 'everybody does everything' so generally accepted in Finland?

Administrative solutions also reflect the bipartite background of the Finnish system. Two ministries, the Ministry of Social Affairs and Health, and the Ministry of Education have the major responsibility for early childhood education and care in Finland. Attached to the ministries are two powerful agencies, which have a direct interest in early childhood matters, STAKES (the national Research and Development Centre for Welfare and Health) and the National Board of Education, which have a direct interest in early childhood matters.

Since, in the Finnish social welfare society day care (ECEC) is seen as a part of the social services offered to families. It comes administratively under the Ministry of Social Affairs. On the other hand the National Board of Education has been actively developing the core curriculum for the pre-school year (six-year-olds).

The staff of the day-care centres. The tension between education and care is also seen in the multi-professional staff at the day-care centres, which mainly consists of kindergarten teachers, social educators and practical nurses. The initial education and training for each group is different and so is their orientation to work. Jarmo Kinos, a Finnish researcher on ECEC policy, has stated that Finnish day care is a field where everybody has to deny her background: a kindergarten teacher has to deny her teacher identity, a social educator her identity as a social worker and a practical nurse her caring identity. This sometimes results in a poor compromise where it is the least common denominator that underpins the work with children. This is far from the goal for multi-professional teams, namely, a situation in which the full potential of everybody is taken into account and used in an ideal way for the benefit of children and their families.

The decline in the initial education and training of the staff is a change that is in sharp contrast to the politically correct talk about high-quality provision of services. Surprisingly, in a country where education is highly valued, the qualification requirements of the staff at the day care centres has been lowered. Previously two out of three staff members who work with children over three at the day care centres had to have training from a polytechnic as kindergarten teacher or social educator. Since 1992 the regulation has been very loose. Now every third staff member has to have training from a polytechnic but there is no statutory definition of what the acceptable degrees are. In practice most of these "third persons" are kindergarten teachers or social educators, but they could actually be engineers as well. The two other staff members are usually practical nurses.

In practice, this loose regulation has meant that the proportion of qualified staff has fallen. At the same time staff with upper secondary level vocational qualification in social and health care has increased (Karila & Nummenmaa 2001, pp. 37-38). The change is even more striking if we look at the relationship between care oriented and pedagogically oriented staff members in that there are less and less kindergarten teachers, who have traditionally been responsible for ECE. There is a sharp contradiction between increasing demands on education and less on resources.

The decline in the qualifications of the staff without doubt present the mainstream, but there are interesting counter-currents as well. Since 1995 kindergarten teachers have received university training at various levels, mostly B.A. This could be seen as a sign of the importance of the educational quality of the staff at the day-care centres. However, in the current situation it is obvious that one improvement is not enough to compensate for the severe erosion of early childhood education due to the decline in educational quality.

The radical deregulation of the early 1990s meant that the autonomy of the municipalities was reinforced. The local authorities are now responsible for providing ECEC and services overseeing. (Karila & Nummenmaa 2001, p. 15; OECD, 2001, p. 42) In the spirit of decentralisation, each municipality develops its own curriculum (for the six-year-olds) or local guidelines for pre-school education (under six-year-olds) taking the local circumstances into account. Each day-care unit and school then develops its own curriculum in more detail. At the unit level, it is recommended that the curriculum be drawn up in co-operation with staff, parents, and children (OECD 2001, p.30).

All of this reflects trust in the competence and motivation of people both at the administrative level and in practice. Nevertheless, there is some support available for construction of the local curricula: a national pre-school curriculum (for six-year-olds) and national guidelines for ECE (children under six) provide the basis for curriculum work. However, it is worth pointing out that both of these documents are very general and offer hardly any support of the implementation phase.

Monitoring the system and evaluating quality. Quality is one of the main topics in the current ECEC discourse in Finland. The importance of quality evaluation is well understood in the municipalities, and directors, teachers, and staff seem well aware of the need to maintain quality in their centres. But how does monitoring and quality evaluation actually work? What kind of data is obtained regularly and analysed? How is information disseminated and shortcomings followed up?

These questions are core questions in every country, but are of special interest in a country like Finland where the national inspection system run by the National Board of Education was abandoned over a decade ago as demoralising and professionally unnecessary (OECD, 2001, p. 42). Does this kind of rhetoric implicitly suggest that we should uncritically trust in the system? Does it also mean that revealing shortcomings in practice is seen as indicating distrust in the competence of the staff? Day care has a very positive image with parents and professionals alike. Does this also prevent us from seeing problems in our system?

One of the concerns of the Review Team was the ill-defined steering and evaluation system in ECEC in Finland. Today STAKES uses 'a light touch' in monitoring and evaluating ECEC after having lost its supervisory role somewhat in the decentralisation process. (OECD, 2001, p. 42) There are numerous projects on quality going on in Finland, but the general picture is still fragmented both regionally and as to substance, e.g., much emphasis is put on client-oriented evaluation understood as the level of satisfaction of the parents, whereas evaluation of the process is neglected.

The team suggests 'a heavier touch', i.e. a more systematic monitoring and evaluation system including development and use of guidance and framework documents like national voluntary standards, codes of ethics, guidelines, recommendations, etc. to direct ECEC policy and services. In addition, judicious use of special funding is recommended to meet the educational needs of local authorities responsible for the quality of ECEC in their region. A new culture of evaluation and quality control is needed. Unless there is regular follow-up, evaluation and steering by municipalities of their own early childhood servi- ces, achievement of goals and improvement will not happen (OECD, 2001, p. 47).

All this suggests that ill-defined adult roles are typical of Finnish ECEC. The 'everybody does everything' policy combined with shift work due to the long opening hours of the day-care centres (e.g., 6.30 a.m.- 18.00 p.m.) leads to situations where it is not the best educated but the least educated who are responsible for the most educationally demanding situations. Kindergarten teachers, especially, seem to have suffered from the erosion of their professio- nal identity: education and care are not in balance on the job.

The work load of the principals of the day-care centres have grown during the last ten years. This has meant more and more administrative work, while their educational leadership has declined. The discourse on 'self-oriented teams' has not solved the problem: it is evident that in the current situation in Finnish ECEC educational support and supervision is also needed on the level of individual settings.

From certain to uncertain child-rearing practices. The change in child rearing practices makes the situation even more challenging. The unquestioned authority of parents have broken down and the strict discipline have made way for permissive attitudes. At the same time child-rearing practices have changed from certain to uncertain. In a perspective of 40 years one can see this trend clearly in Finland: emotional democracy (Giddens, 1995, p. 261) and pall parents are new trends which contrast with the more traditional solid roles of parents. However, the emotional democracy not only means taking children's needs into account, but also demanding decision-making at an early age. Parenthood is said to be lost: parents are half adults (Bly, 1996) who seek immediate satisfaction just as young children do. Through endless negotiations parents try to coax the children to do voluntarily what they want them to do in order to save the children from disappointments which characterise life (Kalliala, 1999, pp. 26-30).
Do these tendencies mean a change towards the better or the worse from the child's point of view? One can evaluate contemporary childhood and that of yesterday from many perspectives even when the findings are similar. For example, the 'poor child' (Dahlberg, 1997) gets a different stigma depending on the meaning given to certain child-rearing culture of the 50s with the inner- directed character (Riesman, 1952) as its ideal. Was the child pushed into passive 'poverty', to wait for occasional attention from adults or did adults accept the

neediness of the child, understanding that the child could succeed with the help of adults? Was the child forced into the margins or was he released from making decisions too heavy for him? Did 'marginal' mean a safe space and time for the unhurried growth of the child? Did the clear boundary between adulthood and childhood mean in the first place security or domination?

Analogically, interpretation also makes a difference when childhood of today is evaluated. Does the idea of a 'competent' and 'rich' child mean demands for a precocious and self-satisfied competence or the permission to fully flourish? Does 'emotional democracy' mean listening to the child and taking into account the child's needs or putting the responsibility of the decision making on the shoulders of the child? Does 'the inner hero as an obligatory paradigm' (Siltala, 1996b) oblige even young children? Is the post-modern child responsible for constructing his own identity? Is the child supposed to construct his own childhood?

It is evident that the sign might change from minus to plus when evaluating childhood in the 50s as well as today. It is also evident that the problems tend to concentrate in different places: when the child of the 50s faced the risk of being restricted by unambiguous rules, the child of today might suffer insecurity because there are no clear rules.

One can, of course, try to construct a model that would guarantee the good of the child in a value-based and ideal manner, both in the context of the 50s and in the current context. The certain and steadfast child-rearing practises of the 50s were certain only to the extent and concerning the aspects which would support the child while uncertain child-rearing practices of today are uncertain only to the extent and concerning the aspects that would mean listening to the child and offering an ideal space for the child's own ideas.

On the other hand one has to ask how many parents are able to live up to this kind of parental role based on a mature and trustworthy concept of adulthood at a time when the obscurity of the boundary between adulthood and childhood has raised the question of whether 'education disappears and adulthood faints' (Hoikkala, 1993).

Thus, the uncertain adult roles at the day-care centres are in tune with uncertain adult roles beyond this setting. In this cultural context the widely-accepted ideas of child-centred and child-initiated education or the constructivist view of learning have not offered a solution to the dilemma of ideal adult roles (Tahkokallio, 1999, pp. 21-25). Long maternity leaves and beautiful settings and good adult-child ratios do not save the situation - according to the latest research findings, the emotional well-being of Finnish children is frightening low (Bardy, Salmi & Heino, 2001).

2 Part 2

2.1 Involvement as a tool for professional development

In this part of the article the adult role is examined in the research context.

2.1.1 THE FRAMEWORK AND GOALS OF THE STUDY

This study arises out of a framework of self-improvement that encompasses a process-oriented and inclusionary commitment to quality evaluation and improvement (Laevers, 1993; Pascal, 1993; Mould, 1998). The quality of practitioners and the self-awareness of the staff f has been shown to be crucial to improving practice. (Blenkin et al., 1997; Kärrby et al., 1995) How, when and under what conditions teachers learn are of supreme importance (Day,1999).

The aim of this research is to

1) explore the potential to enhance the effectiveness of early learning experiences for young children as a consequence of genuine collaboration between the researcher and the teacher.

2) explore the potential of the study as a form of personal and professional development.

This is part of an international study in which personal professional experiences are shared by British (Dr. Claire Mould) and Finnish teams.

2.1.2 RESEARCH OUTLINE

The study arises from the action research paradigm. The first cycle of the study started with evaluation in November 1998, and progressed through the action planning and development phase to final reflection in June 1999. The second cycle proceeded November to the reflection phase in June 2000. Four kindergarten teachers from four day-care centres in the Helsinki metropolitan area in Finland were involved in the research. The day-care centres represented a diverse geographical and socio-economic spread. The teachers were selected because they showed interest in improving their practice with the researcher.

Each teacher chose a sample of five "target children". Two of the teachers chose their sample among four-year-olds and the other two from among five-year-olds. I asked them to choose children who were typical of the group and whom they felt would be most useful to monitor in terms of the teachers' professional development.

The **third cycle** of the research continued in 2000-01 with two of the teachers.

2.1.3 METHODOLOGY

Throughout the fieldwork both quantitative and qualitative forms of gathering information were utilised. The data consisted of

- systematic observations of the target children (The Child's Involvement Scale) and the teachers (Adult Engagement Scale)
- teacher biographies and interviews
- parent and child interviews
- research journals kept by the teachers and the researcher

2.2 Systematic observations

Two quantitative measures focusing on the process of learning were used :

The Child's Involvement and Adult Engagement. Child Involvement refers to the way the child becomes engrossed in the process of learning, as developed by Laevers (1994), while Adult Engagement is demonstrated by the teacher supporting and facilitating the child's learning (Pascal, 1995).

Laevers defines this concept of child involvement as "a quality of human activity, characterised by concentration and persistence, a high level of motivation, intense perceptions and experiencing of meaning, a strong flow of energy, a high degree of satisfaction and based on the exploratory drive and basic developmental schemes (Laevers, 1993)."

The Child Involvement Scale is an observation instrument intended to measure the level of a child's involvement in an activity. Involvement levels are deduced from the presence or absence of a number of involvement signals which include; concentration, energy, complexity and creativity, facial expression and posture, persistence, precision, reaction time, verbal utterances and satisfaction. The level of a child's involvement can be graded on a scale from one to five. One means no involvement and while five means intense involvement (Laevers, 1994).

The level of Adult Engagement describes the nature of the adductive relationships between the adult and child. Laevers identified three categories of adult behaviour: sensitivity, intervention, and autonomy. The EEL Project team at Worcester further refined the scale and developed the concept of Engagement, defining it as "a set of personal qualities which describe the nature of educative relationships between adult and child. These personal qualities will affect an adult's ability to motivate, extend, enhance and involve children in the learning process. An adult's actions may therefore be categorised as displaying "engaging or non-engaging qualities (Pascal et al., 1995)." It focuses in particular on the sensitivity of the adults to the children, the style of the adult's stimulations and the degree of autonomy they encourage.

2.3 Teacher biographies and interviews

At the beginning of the process the teachers wrote their professional biographies including their training, professional experience and development and future career aspirations. I interviewed the teachers and the parents of the target children. I also talked with children and interviewed them during the process. The interview schedules were developed from the 10 dimensions of quality (Pascal et al., 1995) and provided the framework for the conversations. The aim was to provide an all-round perspective of the practice of the day-care centres.

2.4 The researcher's role

My role as a researcher throughout the cycle was to work collaboratively with the teachers. The cycles included:

1998-1999

- observe level of Adult Engagement and Child Involvement
- collect and analyse data (interviews, observations)
- discuss and evaluate analysis with the teacher
- feed evaluation into planning and practice
- repeat observations and teacher interview
- analyse, evaluate and talk with teacher

1999-2000

- observe level of Adult Engagement and Child Involvement
- analyse data, discuss and evaluate analysis with teacher and her team
- feed evaluation into planning and practice
- repeat observations and teacher interview
- analyse, evaluate and talk together with teacher and her team

2000-2001

- discuss and analyse observations done by teacher and her team
- feed evaluation into planning and practice
- discuss their findings with teacher and her team
- repeat teacher interview

2.5 Results

LEVELS OF CHILD INVOLVEMENT

The levels of child involvement rose in all day-care centres during the research process 1998-1999.

Table 1: Levels of Child Involvement in 4 day-care centres in 1998-1999 (5- point scale)

Day-care centre	Level of involvement		The rise of involvement autumn - srping
	Autumn	Spring	
1	3.090	3.530	0.440
2	3.790	3.893	0.103
3	3.432	3.673	0.241
4	3.320	3.795	0.320

The rise in involvement was highest in day-care centre 1, which is situated in an area where many children come from problematic socio-economical backgrounds.

The levels of child involvement rose in all day-care centres during the research process 1999-2000.

Table 2: Levels of Child Involvement in 4 day-care centres in 1999-2000 (5- point scale)

Day-care centre	Level of involvement		The rise of involvement autumn - srping
	Autumn	Spring	
1	3.249	3.580	0.231
2	3.466	3.650	0.184
3	3.459	3.650	0.190
4	3.639	3.859	0.220

Day-care centre 1: the group of children changed completely. During '98-'99 there were 22 children, 14 Finnish and 8 from different cultures. During 1999-2000 there were 15 children from 7 different cultures (Indian, Somalian, Angolan, Pakistan, Russian and 1 Finnish).

Day-care centre 2: the group of children partly changed and target children changed completely. One adult in three changed.

Day-care centre 3: the group of children changed partly. The target children stayed the same. Of three adults only the kindergarten teacher was the same.

Day-care centre 4: the group of children changed partly. The target children stayed the same. One adult in three changed.)

LEVELS OF ADULT ENGAGEMENT

Table 3: Levels of Adult Engagement in 1998-1999 (5- point scale)

	Level of adult engagement		The rise of adult engagement
	Autumn	Spring	autumn - spring
Sensitivity	3.798	4.104	0.316
Stimulation	3.636	3.879	0.243
Autonomy	4.132	4.070	-0.062

The level of sensitivity rose most, by .316 , while stimulation rose by .243 and autonomy fell a little on the five point scale.

Table 4: Levels of Adult Engagement in 1999-2000 (5-point scale)

	Level of adult engagement		The rise of adult engagement
	Autumn	Spring	autumn - spring
Sensitivity	4.145	4.057	-0.088
Stimulation		3.852	3.805 -0.047
Autonomy	4.191	4.128	-0.063

There were very small changes. They have to be interpreted individually in connection with the composition of the group of children.

LINK BETWEEN INVOLVEMENT AND ENGAGEMENT LEVELS

Laevers (1994) and Pascal & Bertram (1995) have shown that the involvement levels have much to do with the qualities of the teacher, but they also remark that the composition of the group of children has an effect on the achievement of high levels.

I would like to study the case (day-care centre 1), in which the increase in the level of involvement was highest more closely. In this case the changes in the level of engagement were as follows (during first cycle):

Table 5: The levels of Adult Engagement in day-care centre 1 during the research process 98-99 (5-point scale)

	Level of adult engagement		The rise of adult engagement
	Autumn	Spring	autumn - spring
Sensitivity	3.610	3.961	0.351
Stimulation	3.740	4.230	0.490
Autonomy	4.300	4.115	-0.185

Day-care centre 1 was also the setting in which the level of involvement was lowest in autumn and where there were some problems with the emotional well-being of the children (although they were not children with special educational needs). Four of the five children got more than .50 (.50, .59, .62, .65) increase in involvement. One girl in this group, whose involvement dropped by .16, had an emotionally problematic situation (her father died) .

The teacher of this group writes:

I started conscious observation. I crouched down both in a mental and physical sense. I started to associate with the children in a different way.
And she said:
... this should be self-evident – this observation – but I think this is not so self evident , there are so many levels...
...I have really tried to find out what is happening inside the child.

2.6 The teacher reflected on her observations

Concerning Arto (boy) I really thought this child initiative and giving autonomy and involvement, and how much, when working together is so difficult....

When I found lack of involvement I tried to give them external and social support as much as possible. I arranged the learning environment –less and less preventing the children from doing what they liked to do – I looked for building material for play ... music... clothes for role-plays...built the cottage with the children.... And I carefully saw to it that Arto and Kalle didn't rush upstairs to play...

Arto's level of involvement rose from 2.812 to 3.400 between autumn and spring.

In this group the children had problems with peer-relations. Some parents talked about the tendency of girls to reserve friends. One mother said:

Ista has problems with friends, she feels tense about it — I think that it is a lot of the children's shoulders. I suppose these adults think that Ista has to walk that way, she has to learn to cope.

In my observations I found that plays and games came to an end very quickly. Promising action was often interrupted by quarrels.

2.7 In June [1999] the teacher reported

I am very satisfied that I had the courage to interfere in the friend-reservation system – it was quite a cruel, hard game...... The parents seemed to be very happy, it has bothered children in the evenings at home.
The rise in Ista's involvement rose from 3.411 to 4.076 between autumn and spring.

We reflected on the balance of these engagement variables and the characteristics of the children and our conclusion was that autonomy was too high for these children .

When we analysed the changes in the levels of Involvement and Adult Engagement in June, the teacher said:

You could say I kept my light under a bushel. I tried to keep myself smaller so as not to smother the children, and kept my ego in the background. Yes, I know I have good charisma, but the important thing is how to use it and the responsibility [1999].

...I learned that my own engagement is the crucial factor [1999].

...in Arto's case I was thinking what child-initiative pedagogy is and so on. I think the adult should see the children's needs, no matter if it is child-initiative pedagogy [1999].

...last year I thought I was being very child-oriented, but actually I guess I was very adult-centred. Now, as I've started to sort of use a little more authority and put myself more into the play, my work has perhaps become more child-oriented and child-centred. You know, at some stage, I was wondering what child-initiative pedagogy really was, and now I've come to the conclusion that the adult's input is enormous, it really matters what the adult does. The mental presence is the most important thing - and that you support the children's activities and are involved in them in that way [2000].

This day-care centre tried to carry out child initiative pedagogy very consciously, basing their curriculum on these principles. Play, art and expression had a very important role in their methods. About 25 % of the children had a multicultural background. The democratic and client-oriented approach is important.

The teacher tried to give space to the children and respect them as autonomous, active people. They had tried to improve their practice by allowing more autonomy; children could choose what they wanted to do (almost always). Negotiating rules was also common.

During the last fifteen years the criticism of adult-centred pedagogy had shown the weak points of " the old pedagogy". It seems evident that adults have interpreted this by distancing themselves from the children without analysing the reality more carefully. The observation of involvement has made it possible to look more closely at the child. This has resulted in a better understanding of what is really happening inside the child. The increase of involvement meant in this case more sensitivity, more activation, less autonomy.

When I compare my own findings with Claire Mould's English data there are some interesting differences:

Table 6: Scores for Sensitivity, Stimulation and Autonomy in Autumn and Spring

	Sensitivity		Stimulation		Autonomy	
	British	Finnish	British	Finnish	British	Finnish
Autumn	4.601	3.798	3.758	3.636	2.968	4.132
Summer	4.732	4.104	4.026	3.879	3.854	4.070

The British figures on Autonomy are much lower at the beginning of the first cycle. In the British material there is a considerable increase in the level of autonomy. By contrast autonomy decreased. In both countries the level of involvement increased, which makes one wonder what the explanation for this discrepancy is.

2.8 Conclusion

The interpretation of findings has to be based on cultural analysis. When, in the British context, the aim is to improve the quality of ECE, it may be appropriate to try to raise the autonomy for the teachers whereas in the Finnish context, increasing the level of involvement may demand more stimulation and less autonomy. This is understandable in the cultural context which consists both of the micro level of the day-care centres and the macro level of general child-rearing practices and ECEC policy. Independence is highly valued in post-modern Western societies but in Finland it has become the value of values. Together with ill-defined adult roles this often leads to leaving the children alone in the name of independence and autonomy.

Figure 1: The optimal relation between the style dimensions

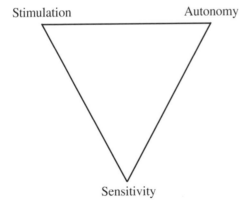

However, in both countries sensitivity is the crucial element if the ideal balance between autonomy and stimulation is to be found. The idea of an ideal balance may be illustrated by a triangle in which the three elements, sensitivity, autonomy and stimulation are at the apices. The special character of sensitivity becomes clear when we make the triangle stand on the point that represents sensitivity: without sensitivity it is impossible to achieve and maintain the balance between autonomy and stimulation.

References

Blenkin, G.M. & Lelly, A. V. (1997). *Principles into practice in early childhood education*. London: Paul Chapman Publishing.

Bardy, M., Salmi, M. & Heino, T. (2001). *Mikä lapsiamme uhkaa? Stakes. Raportteja 263*. Helsinki.

Bly, R. (1996). *The sibling society*. Harmondsworth: Penguin Books.

Dahlberg, G. (1997). *Barnet och pedagogen som medkonstruktörer av kultur och kunskap* (Visible child – Invisible Quality –Conference. 15. – 16.11.1997). Finland: Järvenpää.

Day, C. (1999). *Developing teachers: The challenges of lifelong learning*. London: Falmers Press.

Early Childhood Education and Care Policy in Finland (2000). *Ministry of Social Affairs and Health. Publications 2000.21*. Helsinki: Author.

Giddens, A. (1995). *Reflexive modernization. Politics, tradition and aesthetics in the modern social order*. Cambrigde: Polity press.

Hoikkala, T. (1993). *Katoaako kasvatus, himmeneekö vanhemmuus? Aikuistumisen puhe ja kulttuurimallit*. Helsinki: Gaudeamus.

Kalliala, M.(1999). *Enkeliprinsessa ja itsari liukumäessä. Leikkikulttuuri ja yhteiskunnan muutos*. Helsinki: Gaudeamus.

Karila, K. & Nummenmaa, A. R. (2001). *Matkalla moniammatillisuuteen. Kuvauskohteena päiväkoti*. Helsinki: WSOY.

Kinos, J. (1997). *Päiväkoti ammattikuntien kampppailujen kenttänä. Turku: Turun yliopiston julkaisuja*, sarja 133, Scripta lingua fennica edita.

Kärrby, G., Giota, J., Sheridan, S. & Däversjö-Ogelfelt, A. (1995). *Metod för bedömning av kvalitet i förskoleverksamhet – Forskning och utvecklingsarbete*. Opublicerat manuscript, Göteborgs universitet.

Laevers, F. (1993). Deep-level-learning: An exemplary application on the area of physical knowledge. *European Early Childhood Education Research Journal, 1*, 53 – 68.

Laevers, F. (1994). The innovative project "Experiential Education" and the definition of quality in education. In F. Laevers (Ed.), *Defining and assessing quality in early childhood education*. Leuven: Leuven University Press.

Mould, C. (1998). The influence of researcher-teacher collaboration on the effectiveness of the early learning of four year olds in schools in England. *European Early Childhood Education Research Journal, 6*, 19-36.

OECD Country Note (2001). *Early childhood education and care policy in Finland. Ministry of Social Affairs and health. Sosiaali ja terveysministeriö 2001:10.* Helsinki: Author.

Pascal, C. (1993). Capturing the quality of education provision for young children: A story of developing professionals and developing methodology. *European Early Childhood Education Research Journal, 1*, 69 –80.

Pascal, C., Bertram, A.D., Ramsden, F., Georgeson, J., Saunders, M. & Mould, C. (1995). *Effective Early Learning Research Project: Evaluating and developing quality in early childhood settings: A professional development programme.* Worcester: Amber Publishing.

Pascal, C. & Bertram, A.D. (1995). Involvement and the Effective Early Learning Project: Collaborative venture. In F. Laevers (Ed.), *An exploration of the concept of involvement as an indicator for quality in early childhood care and education.* CIDREE: Scottish Consultative Council on the Curriculum.

Riesman, D. (1952). *The lonely crowd. A study of the changing American character.* New Haven: Yale University Press.

Siltala, J. (1996b). Sisäinen sankari pakollisena paradigmana. *Tiedepolitiikka, 4*, 5-22.

Tahkokallio, L . (1999). Lapsikeskeisyyden ja lapsilähtöisyyden monet tulkinnat. In T. S. Karppinen, A. Puurula & I. Ruokonen (Ed.), *Elämysten alkupolulla. Lähtökohtia alle 3-vuotiaiden taidekasvatukseen* (pp. 21-26). Helsinki: Finn Lectuira.

CHILDHOOD PEDAGOGY: THE IMPORTANCE OF INTERACTIONS AND RELATIONS

INSTITUTE OF CHILD STUDIES, UNIVERSITY OF MINHO, AND CHILDHOOD ASSOCIATION, BRAGA, PORTUGAL

Julia Formosinho

1 Introduction

Since 1996 Childhood Pedagogy Project and other Portuguese university projects joined the Experiential Education Project network (Laevers, 1994); those partnerships had an extensive impact on early childhood education in Portugal.

This chapter reports only a small part of the conceptual work and empirical studies that grew out of the partnership of Childhood Pedagogy Project with the Experiential Education Project network.

Childhood pedagogy is viewed as a process of building a learning community involved in construction and evaluation of learning rather than a process of transmitting information to a group of individual learners. In this community knowledge is actively co-constructed, what means that the process of learning is so important as the learned content.

Childhood Pedagogy Project views teachers pedagogical life in classroom as encompassing integrated pedagogical dimensions, integrated curricular areas (Oliveira-Formosinho, J. & Kishimoto, T., 2002), interactions and relationships with parents, families and community (Whalley, 2001). All those dimensions, areas and interactions are sustained by co-constructed knowledge and by cultural and civic values and beliefs, as represented in Figure 1.

Figure 1: Classroom pedagogy

KNOWLEDGE, CULTURAL, CIVIC VALUES, BELIEFS	INTEGRATED PEDAGOGICAL DIMENSIONS						PARENTS COMMUNITY
	Space and materials	Time	Interaction and relation	Children's observation planning evaluation	Projects and activities	Grouping	
	PEDAGOGY TEACHER'S COMPLEX ROLES AND ACITIVITIES AND THE LEVEL OF PEDAGOGY						
	Language	Personal and social development	Mathematics	Expressive Arts	Motor Development	Civic Development	
	INTEGRATED CURRICULAR DIMENSIONS						

Empirical research has shown that early-years teachers, unlike primary teachers, identify the relations and interactions with their auxiliary and subordinate staff in the classroom, interactions with psychologists and social workers and interaction with mothers and fathers as a specific characteristic of their profession (Johnston, 1984).

Research already conducted in Portugal also shows that the search for quality often leads to the development of new interactions – with auxiliary staff, trainees, parents, primary teachers, other professionals, community agents.

Thus professional development of early-years teachers can be looked at as a process of development of interactions and relations from the micro-level of the classroom to larger levels such as the school and community.

This means that professional development can be viewed as the development of early-years teachers interaction profile. Can initial and in service teacher education programs support teachers in developing adequate interactions profile?

The studies to be reported are centred on the research of interactions as a mean to develop Childhood Pedagogy. The chapter reports research on profiles of interaction (Oliveira Formosinho, 2001a) at the level of experienced teachers (Oliveira Formosinho, 2001b) and new teachers (Oliveira Formosinho, 2001c).

- the first study (Mediation Profile) characterises the performance profile of Portuguese early-years practitioners in comparison to the profile of teachers in other countries, namely the United Kingdom
- the second study is a longitudinal study of 80 pre-school student teachers' interaction styles addressing the possibility of professional growth at the level of interactions styles

This will allow reflection around interactions as a very important dimension on childhood pedagogy. It will allow also advocating the need to consider teachers interaction as a central theme for teacher education programs and as a central professional competence to develop.

2 Mediation Profile Study

2.1 Aims of the research

The study aimed to characterise the performance profile of Portuguese early-years practitioners in comparison to the profile of teachers in other countries, namely the United Kingdom. The study does not envisage to be representative of the level of interactivity of Portuguese early-years practitioners, but just of the dominant style of interaction.

This was conducted not through a national sample, but by creating groups different in those dimensions that research has proved to be central to the quality of the educational services: training and experience. Research into teacher training in general and, specifically, into the training of early-years practitioners has stressed that training throughout the entire professional cycle based on perceived problems, questions and dilemmas is the most effective way of developing professional competence.

2.2 Research methods

The study presented here analyses the performance profile - or the characteristics of the educational interaction – of a group of 62 early-years practitioners divided into three groups. One group consists of trained, experienced teachers (with an average of eight years' experience), who have sustained support for educational practices. The second group benefits from the same sustained support in the field, but consists of less experienced teachers (with around two-and-a-half years practical educational experience). The third group is the same as the first in terms of years of experience, but does not benefit from sustained support in the field.

Two trained observers made the observations - observing children, teachers and early-years education contexts. Both observers underwent specific training in the engagement scale, which involved an inter-observer reliability quotient as a way of checking the reliability of the observations made.

The observations were carried out in the following manner: 1) on two different days, in the morning and in the afternoon, making a total of four sessions per adult; 2) five three-minute observations were made on each day and in each session; 3) after each observation, there was a pause to decide on the classification to be given.

Thus, the total observation per session and per adult took fifteen minutes plus five minutes for scoring. The four observation sessions took up eighty minutes. The observations were recorded on an observation form for adult performance so four observation forms were therefore obtained for each adult observed.

2.3 Main results

The averages of each group on the three sub-scales (sensitivity, autonomy and stimulation) were as follows:

Table 1: Table of averages bij group

Group	Sensitivity	Autonomy	Stimulation
Group 1 (n = 18)	3.82	3.38	3.18
Group 2 (n = 18)	3.91	3.68	3.26
Group 3 (n = 26)	3.66	3.62	3.08
N=62	3.79	3.56	3.17

113

The analysis of these results shows, among other things, that:

- the average for sensitivity on the sub-scale is higher than for the other two sub-scales of autonomy and stimulation. This can be seen for each and all the groups, which means that it is true for the whole group

- the lowest average, for each and all of the groups, is that obtained on the sub-scale of stimulation

- on the autonomy sub-scale each group - and therefore the whole group - presents a higher average than that obtained on the stimulation scale and a lower average than that obtained on the sensitivity scale

A pattern of professional performance is therefore formed, in terms of what we call the characteristics of the educational interaction profile of early-years practitioners. Since this is consistent throughout the groups, it can be hypothesised as being a typical profile of Portuguese early-years teacher.

Figure 2: Mediation profile of Portuguese early years teachers

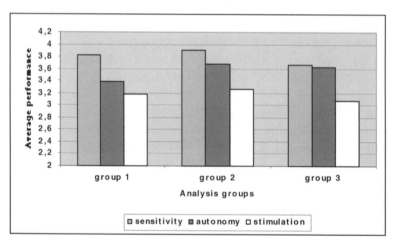

It is curious to note that the English reality is somewhat different. Data collected as part of the EEL Project (Pascal & Bertram, 1999) shows consistently the interaction profile of English early-years teacher: sensitivity – stimulation – autonomy. This is a very different hierarchical configuration of the interaction profile; the Portuguese profile having autonomy as second dimension and the English profile having stimulation as the second dimension.

2.4 Interpretation

In view of this data, it is necessary to reflect upon the Portuguese educational reality. Apart from the differences between groups (which we are not studying), it should be pointed out that all the groups scored higher than the quality definer (3.5 according to the scale creators) in terms of sensitivity and autonomy. All the groups were below the quality definer on the stimulation scale.

One can consider that there are two dimensions that characterise Portuguese early years professional culture. Firstly, respect for the child, reflected in the tone of voice, in the gesture, in visual contact, in listening, in encouragement, in empathy for the child's needs and concerns (measured by the sensitivity scale). Secondly, belief in the child's competence in the area of self-initiated activity: allowing choice, giving opportunities for experimentation, encouraging the child's ideas and the autonomous resolution of conflicts, encouraging one we could say that another characteristic is a certain retraction in terms of stimulation. This can be seen both through the teacher's suggestions and in terms of the activities and information that he/she offers or the manner and content of his/her interventions when he/she enters the child's or group's previous game.

A first interpretation of this data would lead us to say that we are in a early-years culture that centres round the child. The child is respected and given autonomy and this culture is sustained (even implicitly) in an active and Piaget-like view of the school, increasingly distant from theories based on Vygotsky or his followers.

Nevertheless, a second analysis of the pattern of this form of educational interaction may dispute this first analysis.

One of the central concepts of Vygotsky's work (1991, 1993, 1995), which has been increasingly influential in the world of education, is the concept of mediation (Wertsch, 1985). In fact, for Vygotsky, cultural instruments such as language, signs and symbols mediate the development of the higher psychological functions and the specifically human psychological processes. The adult is a dual intermediary in this mediation, since during shared activity he/she teaches the child these instruments and is therefore mediator of the acquisition of cultural instruments which, in their turn, measure the development of superior psychological functions such as voluntary attention and voluntary memory. This is a dual mediation (he/she mediates the acquisition of instruments which, in turn, mediate the development of characteristically human functions). These functions therefore have a doubly social construction: the adult provides access to the cultural instruments which are then necessary in interpersonal interaction to develop the social process of the construction of the specifically human – voluntary attention, logical memory, logical thought, the formation of ideas, the development of will.

If one analyses the characteristics of adult performance (see Appendix), we can see that the adult allows the child to choose and have his/her own ideas, to experiment and assume responsibilities and to make judgements on his/her own work.

In fact, in the language of Vygotsky, this means that, in the area of joint activity, the teacher supports the child in self-planning, monitoring and checking. The teacher gradually gives the child a share in the responsibility of planning, guiding, performing, monitoring, checking and assessing. We are at the heart of meta-cognitive mediation.

We then have to reconsider the first interpretation of the data and say that, in this culture, the presence of Vygotsky can be felt at the level of meta-cognitive mediation, since autonomy is understood here as a form of meta-cognitive stimulation.

By planning, reflecting upon and controlling his/her own actions the child is allowed to develop: he/she has more freedom – free from the field of perception – more flexibility, mediation and free thought. Children and teachers collaborate in the mutual humanisation process.

This brings interactions to the centre of Childhood Pedagogy (Oliveira-Formosinho, 1998). Indeed the importance of child-adult interactions is extensively, recognised in the literature (Bertram, 1996) and can be conceptualised either at micro, meso or macro systemic levels (Oliveira-Formosinho, 2000).

3 Early years teachers professionally – a network of interactions

In this section one analyses early years teachers profession as being based on a network of interactions. The relations and interactions that are required of early-years practitioners at various levels lead to an extended perception of their role.

3.1 A network of extensive interactions

Empirical research has shown that early-years teachers, unlike primary teachers, identify the relations and interactions with their auxiliary and subordinate staff in the classroom, interactions with psychologists and social workers and interaction with mothers and fathers as a specific characteristic of their profession (Johnston, 1984). In fact, apart from requiring all the interaction we have mentioned, early-years education also requires its professionals to integrate services for the children and their families which extends the range of professional interaction. We can therefore say that interaction, at various levels and with various partners, is at the heart of the early-years teacher's professional activity.

Research already conducted in Portugal also shows that the search for quality often leads to the development of new interactions – with auxiliary staff, with trainees, (Lino, 1996), with parents (Oliveira-Formosinho & Andrade, 1996), with primary teachers or even with other professionals and community officials. Thus, the different kinds of interaction with children, with parents, with auxiliary staff, with community leaders, with local authorities, with volunteers, with other professionals, such as psychologists and social workers, represent a unique aspect of the profession of early-years teacher and constitute another factor in this far-reaching role.

The integration of services as a desirable characteristic in early-years education requires the teacher to perform complex roles and functions, to have great understanding and an extensive world of interactions. The capacity for interaction, from within the micro-system of the early-years classroom, to the capacity to interact with all other partners and systems, is essential for the early-years professional. We can thus say that the professional nature of the early-years teacher is located in the world of interaction and he/she develops roles, functions and activity based on this world.

Professional development of early-years teachers is a process that can be looked at as an expansion of interaction and relations from the micro-level of the classroom to larger levels such as the school and community. All these levels influence and are influenced by the macro-levels of national politics and by culture

3.2 The importance of child-initiated interaction – a student-centred process

The specific nature of early-years education can also be seen in the fact that it focuses more on the person being educated – the student – rather than on the educational process or the educator (Silva, 1991). The educational process in early-years teaching is therefore distinct from the educational process of other levels of education, even from the subsequent level of education – primary teaching – because of the importance placed on interaction initiated by the child as the basis or important element of the educational process in kindergartens. An important difference in the models of early-years education, especially for young children, lies in the greater or lesser focus on the child's initiative in developing the educational process.

3.3 The work of the early-years teacher: in the world of interaction

During the 1960s and 1970s, research focused on the effects of the syllabi for early-years education on children at risk[1]. The following decades produced research into early-years practitioners themselves, into initial and on-going training, classroom behaviour and interaction with children.

Although the research has not drawn any clear conclusions, it has produced relevant information on the interaction between early-years teacher and child. Let us look at some studies that clarify these aspects of teacher/child interaction. Philips, McCartney and Scarr (1987), in a study on quality in nine centres in Bermuda, involving 166 children aged between 3 and 6, showed that the amount of time children spent on verbal interaction with the teachers was strongly related to the children's results in the dimensions of language, intellectual development, social competence, sociability and consideration for others.

Holloway and Reichardt-Erickson (1998), in another study, examined not only the amount of interaction time, but also the style of this interaction – for example, the teaching style. They showed that a positive teaching style, characterised as respectful, responsive, engaging and democratic, is associated with the pro-social behaviour of the children in resolving social problems.

The Clarke-Stewart (1987) study also showed that the more directive, controlling and punitive the teachers were, the worse the children did in cognitive development tests and the less co-operative they were with adults. Thus, the teacher's responsiveness (sensitivity and response capacity), the acceptance he/she has of the child and his/her behaviour when providing information, are all linked to the child's competence.

Stipek, Daniels, Galguzzo and Milburn (1992) researched 62 programmes with poor and middle-class children. The instruments used to assess the quality of the contexts and the suitability to development were respectively the ECERS (Early Childhood Education Rating Scale) and the Inventory of Classroom Practices (Hyson et al, 1990). The study also used another instrument designed specifically for this research, which measured the socio-motivational aspects of the children's experience. The analysis of the results led to classification of the programmes based on two dimensions: 1) Positive social climate – measured by the child's initiative, by teacher-warmth and by positive control; 2) Teacher-led instruction – indicated by the academic emphasis, by the pressure to achieve and the stress on assessment.

The most interesting data to come from this study is that it shows that programmes with high levels of teacher direction are invariably the ones that have the lowest level in the assessment of positive social context. As far as this

---

[1] There has been little research into the effects of early-years education on middle-class children.

relationship is concerned, the data is so consistent that the conclusion can be drawn that a great emphasis on academic realisation and on teacher-led instruction seems to impede a positive social environment. In other words, greater emphasis on pre-academic instruction tends to be linked to less emphasis on the positive social relations between teachers and children, which other studies show to have positive consequences (Bredekamp, 1996).

Although there are great difficulties in identifying linear relations between teacher behaviour and the child's developmental results, literature in the field draws great attention to the fact that, once the basic criteria of quality, such as ratio and group size have been established, the most important factors for improving quality are: to train teachers to individualise the teaching-learning process; to stress the child's self-initiated activity; to support the child's development; to create a positive social climate and to encourage parent involvement.

This selection of studies shows how important the teacher's style of interaction is. In fact, the influence of interaction style can be felt both in children at various levels of learning and development (language, intellectual development, social competence, capacity to resolve problems collaboratively), and in the educational environment the teacher creates (the social learning environment).

Figure 3: An ecological image of pedagogy

4 Student teachers mediation profiles: A short-term longitudinal study of student teachers mediation profile

4.1 Research aims

For this context, a fundamental question to be raised is can teacher mediation profile be nurtured? Is it amenable to learning? Can teacher education programs support student teachers in developing their interactions profile? So the fundamental research question is about the possibility of professional growing at the level of engagement style characteristics.

In order to answer a longitudinal research study was conducted with 80 preschool student teachers. The context for this study is the teacher education program of the Institute of Child Studies (University of Minho, Braga, Portugal). An ecological constructivist clinical model for the supervision of early years teachers practicum was established (Oliveira-Formosinho, 2002): it aims to support student teachers professional development through a learning process conducted within classrooms whose teachers have undergone similar professional development processes. So an ecological constructivist clinical model for the supervision is used to build constructivism in classroom practice.

4.2 Research method

The studied group is composed by 80 student teachers taking the professional training that constitutes part of the initial training courses (bachelorship in childhood education), from the Institute of Child Studies from University of Minho, in the school years of 1996-97, 1997-98, 1998-99 e 1999-2000, around 20 students each year. The sample represents a little more than half of the total group of student teachers.

The research to be presented intended to analyse the engagement (interaction style) of the student teachers as central understanding of their mediation profile. This was done in two different moments of their professional training. In fact, student teachers remain in the classroom for proximately four months. This study analyses their engagement, using the already described scale, about a month after the beginning of the professional training and in the end of the training.

To carry on this research the student teacher was video-recorded for about 40 minutes:

- in the period of the daily routine in which she collaborates with the child in the elaboration of child plans or projects
- in the follow up of the development of those plans or projects
- in the sharing, with the child, of comments about the development of those plans or projects

So, the video recording of the student teacher in this period of the daily routine was carried out aproximately one month after her entrance in the classroom and at the end of her training course; then an analysis of this video record was carried out using the engagement scale.

4.3 Results

Table 2:-Moments of evaluation with the engagement scale

Moments of evaluation	Date	Scales used
1st moment n= 80	March/April 1,5 months after the beginning of the training	Engagement scale
2nd moment N= 80	June End of the training	Engagement scale

The observations were carried out by two observers trained in children observation, pre-school teachers observation and early childhood education contexts observation and, specifically, trained in the Engagement Scale.
The use of the video had the advantage of allowing for the reviewing of observation data. A direct observation by sampling was carried out, i.e., the same observers proceeded to a direct observation of one third of the sample aiming at studying possible differences between the observation in video and direct observation. There were no significant differences between the two types of observations.

Table 3: Data presentation

	Sensitivity	Stimulation	Autonomy
1st observation n= 80	3,34	2,79	3,29
2nd observation n= 80	3,69	3,07	3,65

The analysis of this table shows that the mediation profile of the student teacher is lower in stimulation and higher in sensitivity and autonomy, either in the first and in the second observation. The very same profile of experienced teachers. However, the experienced teachers obtained higher averages in all the sub-scales.

Figure 4: Data presentation of Sensitivity, Stimulation and Autonomy

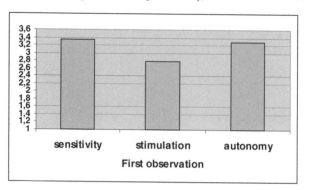

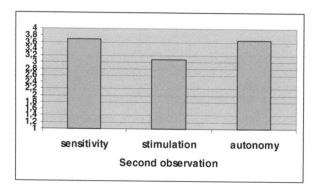

4.4 Interpretation

Taking the data altogether, one can say that:
- from the first to the second observation, the student-teachers mediation profile did change
- the average in all the three sub-scales present gains
- gains were higher in the dimensions of sensitivity and autonomy and last stimulation
- at the level of sensitivity and autonomy, in the second observation, the student teachers present a mean superior to the cut-off point that defines quality practices (3,5)
- in what concerns stimulation, they didn't reach the cut-off point;
- student-teachers present a similar pattern of professional realisation as experienced teachers

Student teachers started with the lowest scores in stimulation sub-scale and had the lowest gains in the same sub-scale. They had support and supervision and couldn't attain the cut-off point. As it was said, this is a profile parallel to the experienced teachers mediation profile in what concerns the hierarchy of the dimensions all though presenting lower averages.

In what concerns the professional cultures, at the level of sensitivity to the child and autonomy granting, we did interpretations in the previously study that can apply for this as well.

We will concentrate now in the question of stimulation. Speaking with student teachers about this, they say that even with support and supervision was already hard to obtain gains at the other two levels and would be nearly impossible to obtain more gains at the level of stimulation without turning to a very didactic style. Indeed, rich stimulation that is developmentally appropriate requires a very flexible and integrated knowledge that is only possible with longer experience, otherwise stimulation can be a transmissive educational strategy.

5 Conclusions

We started with the question of knowing if the mediation profile can be nurtured. Indeed, the data points to the fact that interaction styles can be learned if created the professional development conditions that support growth and development. It highlights also that the time and conditions for the development of the different dimensions of interaction are different. Indeed, reflected experience that allows the student teacher to extend children's ideas and knowledge takes time. This was a very short period (four months) to create the necessary conditions. It is possible to say that teacher education programs and specifically the practicum would gain if they would make interactions a central focus of their professional development aims and activities. The competences for interaction are constructed in interaction.

APPENDIX: Adult Performance

MAXIMUM PERFORMANCE

SENSITIVITY: the adult

- uses a positive tone of voice
- uses positive body language and establishes visual contact
- is caring and affectionate
- respects and values the child
- encourages and praises
- shows empathy with the child's needs and concerns
- listens to and answers the child
- encourages the child to be confident

STIMULATION: the adult intervention

- has energy and life
- is appropriate for the situation
- responds to the child's capacities and interests
- motivates the child
- stimulates effectively and clearly
- stimulates dialogue, activity or thought
- shares the child's activities and focuses on them

AUTONOMY: the adult

- allows the child to choose and supports his/her choice
- gives the child opportunities to experiment
- encourages the child to have his/her own ideas and to assume responsibilities
- respects the child's judgement on the quality of his/her work
- encourages the child to resolve conflicts

MINIMUM PERFORMANCE
(Non-performance)

SENSITIVITY: the adult
- has a negative tone of voice
- is cold and distant
- does not respect the child
- criticises and rejects the child
- shows no empathy with the child's needs and concerns
- does not listen to or answer the child
- talks to others about the child as if s/he were not there

STIMULATION: intervention

- is routine
- lacks energy and enthusiasm
- does not motivate the child
- is not related to the child's interests and views
- is poor and lacks clarity
- is confusing
- is inappropriate
- interrupts dialogue, activity and thought

AUTONOMY: the adult

- does not allow the child to choose or experiment
- does not encourage the child to have ideas
- does not encourage the child to assume responsibilities
- does not let the child judge the quality of his/her work
- is authoritative and dominating
- applies rules and limits strictly and with no room for negotiation

References

Bertram, A. D. (1996). *Effective educators of young children: Developing a methodology for improvement*. Doctoral Thesis, Coventry University.

Bredekamp, S. (1996). Early childhood education. In J. Sikula (Ed.), *Handbook of research on teacher education* (pp. 323-347). New York: Macmillan.

Clarke-Stewart, K. A. (1987). Predicting child development from child care forms and features: The Chicago study. In D. A. Philips, *Quality in child educare: What does research tell us?* (pp. 21-41) Washington, DC: National Assotiation for the Education of Young Children.

Formosinho, J. (2001). The specific professional nature of early years education and styles of adult/child interaction. *European Educational Research Journal, 9*, 57-72.

Holloway, S. D. & Reichhart-Erickson, M. (1988). The relationship of day care quality to children's free-play behavior and social problem-solving skills. *Early Childhood Research Quarterly, 3*, 39-53.

Hyson, M. C., Hirsh-Pasek, K. & Rescoria, L. (1990). The Classroom Practices Inventory: An observation instrument based on NAEYC's guidelines for developmentally appropriate practices for 4- and 5- years-old children. *Early Childhood Research Quarterly, 5*, 475-494.

Johnston, J. (1984). Problems of prekindergarten teachers: A basis for re-examining teacher education practices. *Journal of Teacher Education, 35* (2), 33-37.

Laevers, F. (Ed.) (1994). *Defining and assessing quality in early childhood education*. Leuven: Leuven University Press.

Lino, D. (1996). A intervenção educacional para a resolução de conflitos interpessoais: Relato de uma experiência de formação da equipa educativa. In J. Oliveira-Formosinho (Coord.), *Educação pré-escolar: A construção social da moralidade* (pp.75-103). Lisboa: Texto Editora.

Oliveira-Formosinho, J. (1998). *O desenvolvimento profissional das educadoras de infância: Um estudo de caso*. Dissertação de Doutoramento em Estudos da Criança, Universidade do Minho, Braga.

Oliveira-Formosinho, J. (2001a). The specific professional nature of early years education and styles of adult/child interaction. *European Early Childhood Education Research Journal, 9*, 57-72.

Oliveira-Formosinho, J. (2001b). A profissionalidade específica da educação de infância e os estilos de interacção adultos-criança. In J. Oliveira-Formosinho, & J. Formosinho (Orgs.), *Associação Criança: Um contexto de Formação em Contexto* (pp. 80-103). Braga: Livraria Minho.

Oliveira-Formosinho, J. (Org.) (2001c). A interacção educativa na supervisão de educadores estagiários: Um estudo longitudinal. In J. Oliveira-Formosinho, (Org.), *A supervisão na formação de professores I: Da Sala à Escola, Colecção Infância* (vol. 7) (pp. 121-143). Porto: Porto Editora.

Oliveira-Formosinho, J. & Andrade, F. (1996). O Projecto Infância na sala da Carvalhosa. *Noesis, 39*, 34-36.

Oliveira-Formosinho, J., & Formosinho, J. (Orgs.) (2000). *Associação Criança: Um contexto de formação em contexto.* Braga: Livraria Minho.

Oliveira-Formosinho, J. & Kishimoto, T. (2002). *Formação em Contexto: Uma estratégia de integração.* São Paulo: Pioneira Thompson Learning.

Pascal, C., & Bertram, T. (1999). *Desenvolvendo a qualidade em parcerias: Nove estudos de caso.* Porto: Porto Editora.

Philips, D. A., McCartney, K., & Scarr, S. (1987). Child care quality and children's social development. *Developmental Psychology, 23* (4), 537-543.

Silva, I. L. (1991). Uma experiência no âmbito da formação de educadores de infância. In A. Estrela, M. Pinto, I. L. Silva, A. Rodrigues & P. Pinto (Coords.), *Formação de professores por competências – Projecto Foco* (pp. 49-79). Lisboa: Gulbenkian.

Vygotsky, L. S. (1991). *Obras escogidas I.* Madrid: Ministério de Educación y Ciencia.

Vygotsky, L. S. (1993). *Obras escogidas II.* Madrid: Ministério de Educación y Ciencia.

Vygotsky, L. S. (1995). *El desarollo de los procesos psicológicos superiores.* Barcelona: Crítica.

Whalley, M. & The Pen Green Centre Team (2001). *Involving parents in their children's learning.* London: Paul Chapman Publishing.

Wertsch, J. V. (1985). *Vygotsky and the social formation of mind.* Cambridge: Harvard University Press.

ENABLING AND EMPOWERING EARLY INTERVENTION PROFESSIONALS – A REFLECTIVE PRACTICE BASED ON EXPERIENTIAL EDUCATION

Gabriela Portugal, Paula Santos

1 Introduction

Early Intervention (EI) is a program for children under 3, with a handicap or at risk of serious developmental delay, and their families, aiming to support and promote the well-being and physical, social, emotional and cognitive development of children. It involves services, in every district of the country, belonging to different State Departments (Education, Health, Labour and Solidarity) permiting the creation of multi-professional teams, working collaboratively at a local level. From this local level team emerges an interventionist who works directly with the family (the key-person for the family). According to the legislation concerning EI, published in 1999, in each district of Portugal, there's a coordinating team, who has the role of planning, supervising and evaluating the development of EI on their geographic area of coordination.

In this context, the *Universidade de Aveiro – Departamento de Ciências da Educação*, was asked to participate in the *Projecto de Intervenção Precoce de Aveiro*, at the level of the district coordinating team (joining Health, Education, Labour and Solidarity Departments). EI in the Aveiro district includes nineteen counties, mobilizing around two hundred professionals from several disciplines and agencies, integrating the local counties' teams, and attends nearly four hundred at risk children and their families.

Figure 1:

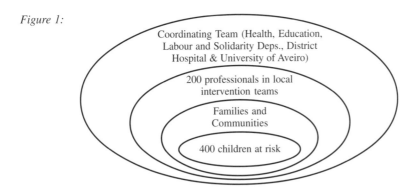

Coordinating Team (Health, Education, Labour and Solidarity Deps., District Hospital & University of Aveiro)

200 professionals in local intervention teams

Families and Communities

400 children at risk

Within this structure, Aveiro University is expected to give guidance to the project, based on quality standards (electing a model), assuring training (according to the elected model - a family centred model), and creating the research mechanism that provides indicators for self-formative evaluation and for the evaluation of the EI impact in the field.

Government policies have not only made monitoring and evaluation a very important element in EI programs but also, implicitly, are committed to "evidence-based" practice. Initiatives such as an EI program, providing support for families and children at risk, promoting well-being and development, and as a long term objective preventing an increase in future personal, social and economical problems, have to be based on measurable outcomes. Today we are seeing an increasing emphasis on using research evidence as a basis for policy and practice change. The notions of "what works", "why" and "what is worth doing," for children seem to be important key-notions for researchers and evaluators (Glass, 2001).

Practitioners who provide and deliver children's services in the community and family find themselves under strong pressure; demanding references and support to develop the relational process underlying EI. Thus, undoubtedly, it's important to have a robust conceptual model as a guiding framework for training, supervision, evaluation and interpretation of evidence.

For the moment we are focussing on training and supervision, in order to enable and empower early intervention professionals. An experiential approach for EI is our option.

2 From relationships to development...

Parents and other caregivers have long known that babies thrive when they receive warm, responsive caregiving and that learning takes place in the context of important relationships. The best way to help very young children to grow into curious, confident, able learners is to provide them warm, consistent care so that they can form secure attachments to those who care for them. Both quality of care and security of attachment affect children's later capacity for empathy, emotional regulation and behavioural control.

But, while rich and positive experiences have positive effects on emotional well-being and the development of children - increasing their resilience -, negative experiences (maternal depression, substance abuse, institutionalisation, chaotic homes, neglect or abusive caregiving relationships...) are commonly

130

associated with higher rates of pre-school and school-aged behavioural and learning problems. Many of those adverse experiences are associated or exacerbated by poverty. Despite the adverse effects of poverty a minority of children appear to thrive: research indicates that among the protective factors that make these children more resilient than others a secure attachment with caregivers seems to be the most important (Egeland, Carlson and Sroufe, 1993). Critical factors that seem to enable adults to care well for their children even in the face of poverty include understanding of child development, social and psychological support.
Families at risk that benefit from social supporting networks seem to be more able to maintain a balanced and caring environment for children, therefore facilitating their development.

There is no doubt that while all parents can benefit from useful information and adequate support as they raise their children, some need more intensive assistance. Efforts to support and strengthen the families, seem to have "protecting" characteristics, as they facilitate family well-being and development. Consistent, well conceived, timely intervention (the earlier the better) can improve the future of many children considered to be at risk of cognitive, social or emotional impairment. Effective intervention can even ameliorate situations frequently thought to be untreatable when genetic disorders or neurological problems are in presence, such as autism, mental retardation or other situations usually labelled as "special educational needs" (Shore, 1997).

3 Early Intervention

The importance of Early Intervention (EI) for young children with disabilities and those at risk has been well established in the last decade. The investment in EI has changed over time, giving place to different EI models (Espe-Sherwindt, 2001; Correia & Serrano, 1998), not always mutually exclusive:

(a) Professional centred – the intervention is focused on the child and decisions are taken by technicians; as they possess the knowledge and expertise required. The professionals know what's best for the child. The family is confronted with its incompetence and ignorance and dependency is installed.

(b) Allied with the family - the intervention is focused upon the child but a contract is established with the family: parents participate in activities that are thought to be important for the child's development... But it's the professional who decides how and what activities are going to be implemented with the family...

(c) Family focused - the intervention is focused upon the family. But there is no real collaboration and acceptance of the family's values, interests and references. In fact, the professional wishes all the families to be alike, their needs and goals matching with the needs and goals elected by the professionals. Most of the time, professionals are trying or wishing to change families in order to get families like their owns...

(d) Family centred – collaboration with the family in the context of development of positive, respectful and equalitarian relationships. It includes mutual problem-solving and shared decision-making.

While there may be substantial variability in the nature and approach of services from one setting to another, today two features can be found consistently across EI programs (Doan-Sampon, Wollenburg and Campbell, 1999; Espe-Sherwindt, 2001). One of these is the emphasis placed on individualising interventions by addressing child and family needs in the form of a personalised family plan. The second feature is a recognition of the importance of involving families across all program dimensions:

- assessment: gathering and recording information;
- decision-making: determining functional goals and objectives;
- implementing intervention;
- monitoring program – assessment;
- determining new goals.

Working and visiting families and young children at risk of developmental delay, frequently dealing with severe situations of poverty and sickness, often evokes significant emotional responses from service providers, challenging their personal beliefs and values, and requiring them to use skills that may not have developed through study or previous work experiences (Copa et al., 1999). The positive impact of the intervention depends on the processes lived by the family, on its desire to become capable, empowered, with a sense of control over its own life, raising their children, participating in the communities they live in, experiencing feelings of emotional well being and involvement. The experience indicates that giving the support worker the opportunity to reflect on the work, thinking and talking about the interactions with children and families, in the psychologically comfortable and secure context of group meetings under a supervisor's guidance, is crucial for the success of the intervention.

Paula: *Since I started to work in EI projects, I felt that my initial training and disciplinary background did not prepare me to work with families – definitely, not in a family centred way; and I've heard many, many times other EI profes-*

sionals complaining about the same. My experience of 10 years as home visitor, trainee and trainer, supervisee and supervisor in the field of EI - working with children under 3 at risk of developmental delay and their families -, taught me most important things in my life, in both professional and personal dimensions. Essentially, I felt the need to see, think and feel as if I was the family of the special needs' child I was interacting with. I always felt a desire to empathise with the family, in such a way that it would become possible for me to share whatever I knew that could be felt as useful by the families, and to understand their knowledge about life, parenting, being part of a community... During all this time, first as a home visitor and supervisee, and later also as a supervisor, I learnt to value the capacity of being a good listener, discovering the forces and positive factors of the families, trusting, recasting what people tell us, enriching it with something new...

I believe it's difficult for us to go over the gap between our traditional way of being educators, in models where the power, the opportunities for making decisions, are very much in the hands of the professional, and very little in the hands, heart and head of the client, whether he/she is a child, a family or a community.

When I met the work developed by the Centre for Experiential Education (Leuven – Belgium), the so called EXE, I felt comforted and excited! It represented the framework I needed to fit what I've learnt during my previous experiences as student, trainee, teacher and person; the conceptual model of EXE permitted to integrate the knowledge and experiences I've had had and all the ones I got from that moment on, acting as foundation and scaffolding the construction of me as a person and professional".

4 Early Intervention (EI) and Experiential Education (EXE)

The core of EI is common to EXE: empowering and enabling the "client" to grow and develop, experiencing feelings of emotional well being and involvement. In both fields, too, there's a reflecting effect: if we want to promote confidence, to empower and enable someone else, we need to be confident, empowered and capable ourselves.

The EXE model appears as a framework that offers a more respectful way of feeling, thinking and doing things in Early Childhood Education (ECE) – a "child centred" way, where the adult pursuits, as point of reference, the child's experience, reconstructing, through his/her expression, word, gesture..., his/her meanings, basing the intervention on child initiative (autonomy), an enriched environment (stimulation) and developing an experiential dialogue (sensitivity), promoting emotional well-being and involvement of the child, and having as ultimate goal the child's emancipation (Laevers & Van Sanden, 1997; Laevers, 2000).

Those core concepts of EXE give light to EI core concepts (Doan-Sampon, Wollenburg and Campbell, 1999) and can be seen as completing each other:

- **family centred** - It means intervention is guided by the family. Family guided intervention follows the family's lead in order to respect not only the child's development but also the family's definition and perception of important developmental issues.
- **ecological** - The EI addresses the broader context of family and community, considering that the different ecological levels interact and influence each other and cannot be treated in isolation. Family culture and environment influence the selection of goals for intervention and the means for reaching the goals.
- **focused on relationships** - Parent-child interactions are the heart of EI. Parents and children may experience difficulty relating. The challenge in such circumstances is to find and nurture the interactive patterns that are adequate and satisfying and then attempt to facilitate an increase in their occurrence so they can compete with and replace less satisfying transactions. A trusting relationship between EI professional and family is also crucial.
- **based on strengths** - The EI process is not intended to intrude upon or judge the family's patterns of interaction. The role of the professional is to join with the family in finding capabilities and interactive strengths, provide needed information and support the family's efforts to optimize their child's developmental outcomes and their individual competence in their parenting role.
- **reflective** - Recognition of the complex system of variables intervening in EI means that the interventionist must gather information over time about the child, the interactions within the family and the environment. Ongoing communication and reflection insures the flexibility and fluidity of intervention as new information is incorporated into the family plan according to the changing priorities and perceptions of the family.

5 Supporting early intervention through reflective practice

In the world of professional practice with young children and their families supervision provides regular opportunities for professionals, less experienced and more experienced, to reflect together about their professionals situations. Just as families need support, information, attention and respect in order to become confident and more competent, professionals need supportive relationships taking the form of supervision, in order to become empowered and capable. As Fenichel (1999) highlights an effective supervision includes some essential features: reflection, collaboration and regularity.

"Reflection can be thought of as both the means and the end of the process of supervision. Reflection involves stepping back from the immediate, intense experience of hands-on work... The supervisor offers an enlarged perspective, another pair of eyes, a mirror... Part of the process of developing a professional identity involves recognising the need to enlarge one's own knowledge, skills, and sensitivity (p.13)." Reflecting on professional identity involves examining experienced feelings, values and personal theories; in toto, continuing conceptualisation of what one is observing and doing.

Working in a wide range of settings, facing intellectual and emotional challenges can be very troubling. Here, the experience of supervision has been described as like *"having a friend on a difficult journey* (p.14)." This is the main reason why an enduring collaborative supervision relationship, nurturing, rewarding, is a desirable part of any training or work environment (only a few want to travel alone through unknown or obscure territory).

Obviously, the development of a supervisory relationship with the characteristics described above needs regularity (time to reflect, time to collaborate and above all, time to establish a trusting relationship).

Different strategies can be implemented in the context of a supervisory relationship. We select case studies and group discussions (Shulman, 1999), and self evaluation.

Case studies and group discussions

One can learn a lot from practice. Stories, critical incidents, cases are important to narrow the space between theory and practice. In order to support supervisees, supervisors need to know their stories, their perspectives and realities. The discussion of cases in the context of supervision and group meetings permits the stimulation of collaborative analysis; the exploration of complex and messy problems for which explicit theories and simple answers do not exist; the generation and examination of different points of view; the development of problem-solving skills; the development of collegiality and a shared understanding in a community of learners; the stimulation of collaborative reflection and strategic introspection of one's own practice (self-evaluation).

Self-evaluation

One common characteristic of teachers and others social professionals is their difficulty in questioning their practice. Frequently problems are explained by referring to characteristics of children, families, culture, mentalities, school organisation, external programs, government etc., not to the practitioners or professional behaviours. Undoubtedly, they work the best they can and know. In spite of this, it is important to develop a culture of reflection and self-evaluation, of modesty and humility. Students and practitioners must realise the impact of their actions and verbalisations on children and families and understand that if children or families are "difficult ones", disturbing, not interested, the professional has to deal with that as his problem, permanently trying out new approaches and alternatives, respecting and trusting children and families. It's not an external problem, beyond his own control, a problem inherent to the child, family or community, having nothing to do with the professional. There's always something that can be done. Constantly, professionals have to question their performance, considering their characteristics, their style etc.

6 The experiential teacher and the early intervention professional style

The bridge between a child centred ECE practice and a family centred EI practice, becomes more clear when we adopt the Adult Style Observation Schedule (Laevers, Bogaerts & Moons, 1997; Laevers, 2000) as a guide to promote professional and personal development, scaffolding reflection and self-evaluation. The ASOS seems to be a powerful instrument in the process of enabling and empowering professionals to develop a sensitive and stimulating

ASOS ECE DIMENSIONS		EI PROFESSIONAL DIMENSIONS
"Is evidenced in responses which demonstrate empathic understanding of the basic needs of the child such as the need for security, for affection, for attention, for affirmation, for clarity and for emotional support." (Laevers, 2000.)	SENSITIVITY	Understanding, the feelings and thoughts of the families, as if they were their own, and letting families know they are understood and appreciated, creating a space of a trusting relationship,respecting their own values and beliefs.
Is evidenced in "open impulses that engender a chain of actions in children and make the difference between low and high involvement. They include: suggesting activities to children (...); offering materials that fit in an ongoing activity; inviting children to communicate; confronting them with thought-provoking questions and giving them information that cancapture their mind." (Laevers, 2000.)	STIMULATION	Creating opportunities for families to build knowledge about themselves as people (discovering their own and their child's strengths and capabilities), the communities they live in (available resources) and the dynamics capable of supporting their growth and development (actions, strategies or means).
"It means: respecting children's sense of initiative by acknowledging their interests; giving them room for experimentation; letting them decide how an activity is performed and when a product is finished and implicating them in the setting of rules and the solution of conflicts." (Laevers, 2000.)	AUTONOMY	It means supporting family members in their strive to design and implement a life project (defining the aims they want to achieve and the best ways to do it).

attitude and the capacity to promote autonomy. These connect with an ecological and person centred model, a reflective attitude, based on strengths and focussing on relationships.

In the context of individual interactions with families interventionists are supposed to make assessments, determine goals and objectives, implement, monitor and evaluate interventions and thus determine new goals. Sensitivity, stimulation and autonomy are crucial dimensions when involving, respecting and collaborating with families across all the phases of the program.

Considering the *identification of goals for intervention*, we can imagine situations like those described below (adapted from McWilliam & Winton, 1991) and connect them, more or less easily, to stimulation, sensitivity or autonomy dimensions. In fact, reality doesn't fit automatically into an organised and static three dimension model or scheme. Reality is a complex organic all. It goes behind knowledge, often laughing from our partial visions. Often, different dimensions co-exist within the same situation, but maybe one is more prominent than the others. Different perspectives, different contexts, different families lead to different answers. The value of this approach has to do with the potential contribution for reflection, discussion and self evaluation, improving the quality of what is offered to families and children.

The EI professional...	Sens	Stim	Aut
...has an understanding of the culture and value system of the families he/she serves. He/she can accept their values, even when they are in conflict with their own.	x		
...assists parents in identifying goals by using concepts, terms and questions they can readily identify with (e.g., feelings, concerns, daily routines, relationships) rather than professional concepts (e.g., cognitive, gross motor, social or self-help skills).		x	
...refrains from providing advice unless he/she is sure that it is really wanted by the parents.			x
...obtains information about the type, amount, and usefulness of support families receive from informal resources (e.g., friends, extended family).		x	
...obtains information from the parents about long-range goals, hopes, and aspirations for the future (for their child, themselves, and their entire family).		x	
...conveys to the parents that he/she understands and believes what they say to him/her.	x		
...assists the families in summarising what they want for their child, themselves, and work together to come up with a list of realistic goals.			x

Considering assessment of the child, we can try out the same exercise:

The EI professional...	Sens	Stim	Aut
...prepares parents for the assessment of their children, informing them of what to expect, giving them a schedule, assisting them in preparing to meet with other team members).		x	
...attentively and clearly explains the purpose, content and scoring of all assessment tools that he/she uses prior to their administration (in language that is understood by the parents).	x		
...talks with parents throughout his/hers assessment of their children (e.g., explaining the purpose and meaning of test items, commenting upon their child's performance).		x	
...allows the parents to administer test items or asks them for suggestions on how to get the best performance from their children (perhaps by demonstrating for him/her).			x
...takes a parent's word as truth when they tell him/her that a child is capable of performing a skill that he/she has not observed the child doing.	x		
...emphasises to parents what their children can do rather than what they can't do.		x	

7 Conclusion: An experiential model for EI supervision

An experiential attitude in EI is important not only at the level of direct intervention with families and children but also at the level of supervision, meaning being in contact with feelings and thoughts of EI professionals. An adaptation of the EXE's temple scheme (Laevers & Van Sanden, 1997) can help to give light to this idea.

Figure 2: The EXE's temple scheme

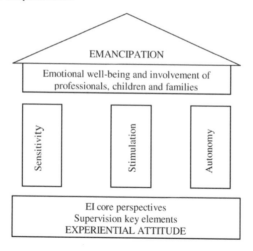

In the context of EI, supervision of key elements like collaboration (resulting from trusting relationships), regularity (consistent time together) and reflection on work, can't take place if the supervisor is not really in touch with the *inner*

experience of EI professionals, paying attention to their feelings and thoughts, rebuilding their experiences, examining the situations and problems through their perspectives. And what does the supervisor intend to promote through his/her interventions? Emotional well-being, specifically confidence, and involvement, specifically a sense of competence and the power to face challenges; in order to attain the emancipation of the main subjects of this process. How can he/she reach these objectives? By being sensitive, stimulating and promoting autonomy in supervisees.

Paula: *As a home visitor to families and children at risk I often felt a strong challenge to my capacities. When working with people and dealing with their problems, we realise very soon that there are no certainties, there's not only one way of doing things. We can simply create the avenue of a nurturing relationship, offering the opportunity for people to choose a way which is the more respectful of their own values and beliefs, so they can be involved and find balance and well-being in their lives. This is not an easy task for a lonely professional. Such a task demands a multi- and transdisciplinary approach. So, the only way I know how to assimilate EI core perspectives, being a family centred, ecological, strengths based, relationship focused and reflective EI professional, is by participating in a reflective group of several people, with different backgrounds, having the same goal and core values, empowered by an experiential supervisor. For me this means a supervisor who empathises with EI professionals' feelings and thoughts, letting them know they are being understood, therefore creating a space of liberty, tranquillity and security, promoting openness to hearts and minds, exposition of doubts, fears or joys experienced while working with children and families. It also means someone who observes and learns with the professionals' knowledge, actively listening to their stories and helping them to built bridges between the problems and the knowledge available in the group, therefore providing a scaffold for a unique emerging transdisciplinary knowledge and understanding. Finally, it means supporting them finding the way to develop their own autonomy, learning how to listen to families, children and colleagues, to evoke knowledge, to link events, assumptions, ideas, and be proactive.*
For me it was crucial to have consistent time together with the elements of my group and supervisor. I needed to know that every week or every two weeks (a larger period of time between meetings brings too much distance from experienced events) I could count on the support of my group and supervisor. This brings an element of balance and tranquillity, too.
In a synergetic effect, I felt that experiencing such a supervision situation enables me to be more sensitive, stimulating and capable of promoting autonomy in families.

I *had been working together with Ana's family – mother and father – for 3 months. We were meeting in a room at our head-office; the parents had declared, at the beginning of our relationship, that they did not want EI support at their home. Ana was improving very well: she had been attaining the developmental tasks we were expecting and, what is more, she was happy, relating to her parents with increased joy, as we could see by her expression, attitudes, movement, and play. Then, at Christmas, the parents told me, "From now on we'd like you to come to our home,... You know, when you asked us what we would prefer, whether to meet at our home or another place, we thought of a brigade, entering our home every week..."*

I felt these parents verbalised what I would feel if I received home visits from some professional I had not known before. I do not believe I would allow an unknown person to come (maybe I should say intrude?) and perform within my home and my family, just like that! Especially if I had already been through difficult situations with "experts" or if I'd been dealing with negative feelings and thoughts about my child' special needs. What would she think about me and my family? What does she know about having a disabled child? How can she judge me?...
I would need to interact with her, to experience relationship situations and, with time, if I feel secure, I would rely on a trusting relationship... It would be important to create a comfortable place for us, where I'd feel at ease, loved, appreciated, valued - even if my own values and beliefs weren't the same as those of the professional interacting with me -, capable and empowered. Under those conditions, I think I would be able to discover whatever my strengths were and to build new ones, in a continuous process of discovering the capabilities and needs of my child, and experiencing those magic, sparkling moments when me and my child really fit in a mutual discovering process of each other, at our best...

Interacting with them and Ana for more than two years, I felt close to them, sharing our strengths, our feelings and thoughts, our doubts,... And we built a project – a dream? – about Ana's well-being and development, their well-being and growth as a family, and my own professional and personal development and well-being. And we gave it life in the every day situations Ana's parents offered her... They found tranquillity relating to Ana and were able to include her, with her capabilities and difficulties in their life project, feeling emancipated...

References

Copa, A., Lucinski, L. & Wollenburg, K. (1999). Promoting professional and organizational development: A reflective practice model. *Zero to Three*, (august/September 1999), 3-9.

Correia, L. & Serrano A. M. (1998). *Envolvimento parental em intervenção precoce. Das práticas centradas na criança às práticas centradas na família* (Col. Educação Especial). Porto: Porto Editora.

Doan- Sampon, M., Wollenburg, K. & Campbell, A. (1999). *Growing: Birth to three. Piecing it all together.* Wisconsin: The Portage Project, CESA 5, Portage.

Egeland, B.E., Carlson, E. & Sroufe, L.A. (1993). Resilience as process. *Development and Psychopathology.* Cambridge: University Press.

Espe-Sherwindt, M. (2001). *O PIAF: Mais do que um pedaço de papel* [Conference and Workshop, Feb. 2001]. University of Aveiro.

Fenichel , E. (Ed.) (1999). *Learning through supervision and mentorship to support the development of infants, toddlers and their families: A source book.* Washington, D.C.: Zero to three, National Centre for Infants, Toddlers and Families.

Glass, N. (2001). What works for children – the political issues. *Children & Society, 15* (special issue: Made to measure ? Evaluating community initiatives for children), 14-20.

Laevers, F. & Van Sanden, P. (1997). *Pour une approche expérientielle au niveau préscolaire. Livre de base.* Louvain: Centre pour un Enseignement Expérientiel.

Laevers, F. (2000). Forward to basics! Deep-level-learning and the experiential approach. *Early Years, 20* (2), 20-29.

Laevers, F., Bogaerts, M. & Moons, J. (1997). *Experiential Education at work. A setting with 5-year olds* [manual and videotape]. Leuven: Centre for Experiential Education.

McWilliam, P. J. & Winton, P. (1991). *Brass tacks.* Chapel Hill: The Frank Porter Graham Child Development Centre, The University of North Carolina.

Shonkoff, J.P. & Phillips, D.A. (Eds.) (2000). *From neurones to neighbourhoods: The science of early childhood development.* Washington, D.C.: National Academy Press.

Shore, R. (1997). *Rethinking the brain. New insights into early development.* New York: Families and Work Institute.

Shulman, J. (1999). Teaching cases: New approaches to the pedagogy of teacher education. WestEd – improving education through research, development and service [Workshop, University of Aveiro, Dec.1999].

WELL-BEING AND INVOLVEMENT AS A GUIDE IN REALISING GOOD CONDITIONS FOR INCLUSIVE EDUCATION IN NICARAGUA

Peter Van Sanden, An Joly

Experiential Education (EXE) has amply proved its worth in the Western educational context. But does this view and its quality concepts also function in the Latin American context, and if so, how? This question has been occupying us ever since we launched an educational project in Nicaragua.

The 'Flemish Organisation for Development Cooperation and Technical Aid' sent us a few years ago to Nicaragua as pedagogical advisors to support the Board of Special Education of the Ministry of Education of Nicaragua in realising their mission, i.e. the development of inclusive education. Strictly speaking, this means the integration of handicapped children in normal education.

Together with our Nicaraguan colleagues we defined two project objectives:

(1) the development of a practical guide on inclusive education in nursery school and elementary school and a corresponding implementation strategy;

(2) the formation of a group of educational advisors who support the process of inclusive education in practice.

In the planning and set-up we explicitly based ourselves on the concepts and instruments developed by the Centre for Experiential Education (EXE) in Flanders. We introduced the children's well-being and involvement as the ultimate quality requirements. The children's education is successful when they are doing well in the setting and when they participate with motivation and intense mental activity. Specifically in reaching the first objective the Process-Oriented Child Monitoring System for Pupils (POMS-P) (Laevers, 1998) and for Young Children (POMS-YC) (Laevers, 2001) is an important source. The POMS is an instrument which helps teachers to find out in time which children are at risk and to systematically work on a care-broadening practice where each child gets what s/he needs for his/her development.
As such, Nicaragua and particularly the Nicaraguan educational situation became our new living and working environment.

143

1 Nicaragua and the Nicaraguan educational situation

Nicaragua, the land of lakes and volcano's, knows peace since 1990, after a turbulent history of wars, dictatorships and revolutions. To the north it is bounded by Honduras, to the south by Costa Rica. To the east and west it forms a bridge between the Atlantic and Pacific Oceans. Nicaragua is the biggest country in Central America and has about 5 million inhabitants, of which 1.4 million lives in the capital Managua. The population is young: 68% of the Nicaraguans is younger than 25, 48% is even younger than 15. Most Nicaraguans speak Spanish, but near the Caribbean coast they also speak English, Creole, Miskito, Rama and Sumo.

Nicaragua is practically the poorest country of Latin America. Despite the recent economical growth, more than half of the population lives below the poverty line. One of the main causes for this is the low level of education, which brings us directly to the educational problems.

A young population, but unfortunately about a million of the children and youngsters do not receive any education at all, while the state schooling is in principle for free. The average Nicaraguan goes to school for only 4.9 years. A Nicaraguan teacher earns on average about 60 U$ per month. Depending on the source, the subsistence level is estimated at about 110 to 180 U$. Hence, many teachers need a second or even third job to make ends meet. In any case, they are not used to working for school after school hours, for example to prepare their classes. Add to this their limited pedagogical and didactical training, overcrowded classes and the dreadful socio-economic situation of the families and one can easily comprehend the reality behind the educational statistics: in 75% enlisted pupils in elementary school only 44.3% reaches the fifth year (MECD, 2002). Only 29 in 100 children complete elementary school within the normal 6 years. In 2001, 18.8% (MECD, 2001) to 35% (UNICEF, 2001) of the population was illiterate. The educational success rate is low, the number of dropouts high.

2 Inclusive education

2.1 Broad interpretation: From the handicapped child to all the children

The Board for Special Education has the ambition to launch inclusive education, i.e. the integration of handicapped children in normal schools. One can ask oneself whether this is justifiable when school is not even evident for children without a manifest handicap? This question is certainly appropriate and this is why we decided to invite the teachers and their advisors to maintain a broad view and not limit their focus to the handicapped children. We want to help them in realising better education for ALL the children. Our aim is to improve the quality of education in general, in order to give children with special educational needs access to the same quality of education. In other words, good normal education constitutes inclusive education, but in the broader sense of the word.

2.2 The children's well-being and involvement: points of reference

The initial question we asked the teachers is: How is EACH of the children doing in the setting? In order to help them answer this question, we gave them two special parameters: the children's well-being and involvement during the classes and activities.

Does the child feel at home in the setting? Does the child feel at ease and can s/he be him/herself in the interaction with me and with his/her peers? Is the child happy? The teacher will find an answer to these questions by focussing on the children's well-being. This will enable the teacher to gain an overall picture of how the child is doing socially and emotionally.

In order to find out whether the child is learning and developing, the teacher assesses the child's involvement: Does the child participate in the classes and activities? And how does the child participate, with intense mental activity and concentration? Does s/he give him/herself for 100%? Is the child enthusiastic and does s/he enjoy the exploration?

If the teacher's assessment for both well-being and involvement is positive, she can conclude that the child is doing well: s/he feels good, is learning and developing. If the child is not doing well for one or both parameters, the teacher knows that something is going wrong.

2.3 Well-being and involvement versus level of competence

We use both parameters in order to find out which children are at risk. These are not necessarily handicapped children. The latter only start having problems when the educational setting (contents, materials, methods, etc.) does not succeed in tuning in to their specific needs, just like for example highly talented children cannot participate with a high level of well-being and involvement if they do not find the mental challenge they need.

Well-being and involvement are not really properties or fixed characteristics of the child itself. They do give an indication of the interaction between the child's characteristics on the one hand and the environment's properties on the other hand. If this interaction is positive, in other words, if the teacher succeeds in tuning in to the child's specific needs, this will result in a high level of well-being and involvement. If the interaction is negative, the setting is not (sufficiently) tuned in to the child's needs, which will result in a low level of well-being and involvement. This explains how even highly talented children can have difficulties.

In other words, involvement is a much sounder criterion to find out which children are at risk than the general level of competence. Competence means the entirety of skills, insights and dispositions that children master at that particular moment.

In order to draw the teachers' attention to this, we invite them to assess every child's level of competence, which means indicate whether the child performs below, on or above the average level of competence of its peers. Teachers often do this spontaneously, linked to the idea that the children with a high level of competence are 'good pupils' while those with a low level of competence are 'weak pupils'. By comparing the results of this assessment with their scores for involvement they can reach a more differentiated conclusion, for example that Danilo is far above the average level of performance, but he is often bored in class, never seems to be mentally challenged, hardly ever reaches a satisfying level of involvement and consequently does not learn at all or at least not enough. Or the other way around, that Rodolfo scores far below the average level of competence, but is very (mentally) active in his (lower) level of development while participating in class and activities (which the teacher has tuned in to his level) and is consequently developing. Or in the case of Walkiria, who is handicapped, but feels comfortable in the setting and reacts in a positive way to the offered opportunities.

Both parameters indicate the core of a broad view on inclusion. It does not mainly involve 'the children with a handicap', but 'all the children with a low level of well-being and involvement'. This view approaches the child's specific characteristics, for example being handicapped, starting from the child's interaction with the setting. It is the quality of this interaction that results in a high, moderate or low level of well-being and involvement. The child with a low level has a problem, not because of its specific characteristics, but because its interaction with the setting is unfavourable. The child does not get what s/he needs and consequently is at risk.

2.4 Well-being and involvement and the issue of quality: The child in the setting with its specific properties

Both parameters complete the quality issue in education by not only focussing on the approach (how is the learning environment and what does the teacher do?) and its effects (to which learning results does this lead?), but at the same time also paying attention to the process, i.e. what happens with the child's perception and mental activity here and now. Moreover, the approach becomes more complete by explicitly focussing on the child's well-being, for we are not only interested in the child's school performance. It is at least as important to pay attention to and care for the child's social and emotional development.

Figure 1: Setting-Process-Effect Scheme

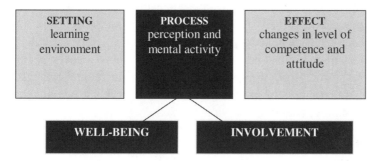

The above-mentioned elements enable us to describe how one can recognise good qualitative inclusive education. Good education means that the teacher succeeds in rising the children's level of well-being and involvement. Good inclusive education means that the teacher succeeds in doing this for ALL the children, regardless of their specific characteristics.

3 Set up and structure of the project

3.1 Action-reflection cycle as a tool

The aforementioned broad view on inclusive education constitutes the theoretical framework that we introduce in the schools for normal education. Implementing this view means creating good conditions in order to let all children with their specific needs benefit from it.

The basic tool that we provide for this is the child monitoring system developed by CEXE (POMS for Pupils and POMS for Toddlers). The POMS and its broad view on the quality of education helps teachers to (1) detect children with extra needs in time; (2) gain insight into the problem and (3) come up with successful initiatives and evaluate them. Our colleagues started calling this instrument the 'action-reflection cycle' (AR-cycle). It stimulates and supports the teachers and their advisors to systematically reflect on their class practice, take actions to improve it and reflect on the result of these actions, etc.

As indicated in the scheme below, the instrument contains a set of 7 forms and additional instructions. By means of this action-reflection cycle, these forms guide the teacher systematically through a first stage of observation, a second stage of analysis and a third and last stage of planning, implementation and evaluation of concrete interventions.

In paragraph 4, we introduce each stage and each form by means of describing how the teachers and their advisors implement them. Soon, it becomes clear that it does not suffice to simply translate the Dutch version of the POMS. It is very important to adapt and document the introduced concepts, forms and instructions starting from the specific Nicaraguan educational context, in other words, making it accessible by contextualising it. Hence, introducing the POMS means translating, adapting and validating it.

Figure 2: Action-reflection cycle

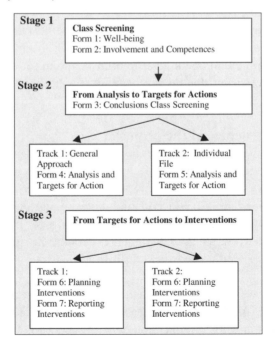

3.2 Structure of the project activities: two components

We spend a considerable amount of time in two pilot schools in the capital Managua; a nursery school (5 teachers, 1 principle) and an elementary school (13 teachers, 1 principle). In both schools we do a small-scale try-out of the instrument, try to explore the teachers' experiences with it, finalise the instructions and forms and record the impact results of its implementation. All this constitutes the project's first component which focuses on the first objective: making a practical guide.

As we are making progress in the pilot schools, we take the obtained results to the 85 advisors who are responsible for supporting the innovation process of inclusion in the schools. Enriched and documented by the experiences and results from the two pilot schools, we support them by teaching them how to implement the same AR-cycle in their supporting role. We also pay attention to aspects of strategic implementation, strategies which enhance a smooth introduction of the AR-cycle. All this constitutes the set-up of the project's second component which focuses on the second objective: training a group of advisors who will help us realise inclusion.

Figure 3: Structure of the project activities: two components

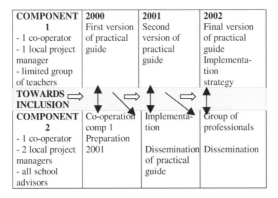

COMPONENT 1	2000	2001	2002
- 1 co-operator - 1 local project manager - limited group of teachers	First version of practical guide	Second version of practical guide	Final version of practical guide Implementation strategy
TOWARDS INCLUSION			
COMPONENT 2	Co-operation comp 1	Implementation	Group of professionals
- 1 co-operator - 2 local project managers - all school advisors	Preparation 2001	Dissemination of practical guide	Dissemination

The work linked to both project components should be viewed against the background of the actual (initial) situation in the pilot schools and the advisors' assignments and tasks. We will describe both in the following paragraphs.

3.3 Initial situation in the pilot schools

Both pilot schools are situated in the poor working class areas of Managua. In the nursery school, five teachers take care of about 170 children between 3 and

6 years old. In the elementary school, 13 teachers are responsible for about 600 pupils spread over six years, from 6 to 12-year-olds.

In both schools we estimate the average level of well-being between moderate and high: the children feel at ease, but they do not radiate. With regard to their level of involvement we estimate a moderate to low score. Most children seem to participate, but show little concentration, energy, challenge, perseverance or mental activity.

A whole range of factors clarifies these levels of well-being and involvement. The classrooms are small, hot and give a rather grim impression: dark colours and little light. Specifically in the nursery school the classrooms are open spaces without corners. The rare didactical and (play) learning material is in a bad shape or totally broken. From the first year in nursery school to the sixth year in elementary school a vertical group teaching method prevails, with little room for individual differences, mainly 'chair and table activities', usually tackling themes or subjects in an abstract way without linking them to reality, very limited opportunities for free initiative, etc.
The teachers mainly focus on the implementation of the curriculum. The interaction with the children is mostly limited to closed questions which are hardly challenging. The teachers are generally friendly and care for the children, however, lack authentic empathy for the children's perceptions. They certainly do not set an exaggerated high level of performance or strict rules of conduct.

3.4 The assignment of the school advisors

Nicaragua counts 25 schools for special education. The Board for Special Education and the MECD have established in each of these schools a so-called Cell for Pedagogical Orientation, consisting of the school's principle and a number of teachers who have received the task of functioning as educational advisors in the process of inclusive education. On a national level, this concerns a group of 25 principles and 60 advisors. Each cell is among other things responsible for organising a psycho-pedagogical test for children who will be transferred to a normal school or a school for special education, closely monitoring the integrated children and supporting their teachers.

Initially, the advisors did not receive clear instructions or instruments. For example, only an obscure centrally developed psycho-pedagogical test existed, which they used with their own inspiration and intuition. The focus of the educational support was limited to the handicapped child and its problems. The advisors did not really visit the teacher, but the integrated child for whom they developed individual monitoring systems which they themselves put into practice by taking the child aside for a while. At the end of such an individual session, the advisor sometimes advised the teacher to implement a certain strategy for further monitoring of the child within the group. As such, 'inclusion' was in fact a completely separate circuit. The child was a member of the group, but isolated on an island.

In the course of the project and with the aid of the AR-cycle, we re-orientate and broaden this focus:

- from the handicapped child to all the children
- from children with specific characteristics to children within the setting (approach) with its specific properties
- from directly supporting the children to advising the teacher who supports the children

4 Practical experiences with the action reflection cycle

The table below shows the training and support scheme after one year of implementing the AR-cycle, from March to November 2001.

Table 1: Training and support scheme

COMPONENT 1 – PILOT SCHOOLS			
	Study and training days	Support sessions at school	Team meetings at school
School A	4	16	4
School B		16	4

COMPONENT 2 – EDUCATIONAL ADVISORES			
	National workshops of 3 days	Regional practical support days	Team meetings at school*
Group A	4	4	6
Group B		4	6

* per group each time for the advisors of a school for special education

We introduced the AR-cycle step by step and this is how we will report it here as well. A description of each stage and of the corresponding forms is followed by practical experiences with (a) the general impact on the teachers and their advisors (what changes within themselves and their practice), (b) how they deal with the concepts and (c) how they use the forms.

4.1 Stage 1: Class screening

Keeping in mind the broad focus, we invite the teachers to make a general assessment of how each child is doing in the setting; for instance how is Luis doing? Does he reach a low, moderate or high level of well-being? How does he participate: with a low, moderate, or high level of involvement? And how about his level of competence: high, moderate or low compared to the group average?

In order to be able to make this assessment, we show the teachers how to pay attention to a range of signals which indicate how the children are doing in the setting. With this information they can fill in form 1: 'Stage 1 – Class Screening: Well-being' and form 2: 'Stage 1 - Class Screening: Involvement and Competence'. The forms provide room for filling in the names of all the children, marking the colour code (red, orange or green) of the corresponding level (low, moderate or high) and adding remarks or clarifications if necessary.

(a) General impact

Both the teachers from the pilot schools and the advisors who present the forms to their respective teachers, indicated that the assignment forces them as it were to do something they are not used to doing, i.e. explicitly focussing their attention on the children, what's more to ALL the children. We can understand this reaction, since the teachers are mainly worried about implementing the obligatory curriculum accurately, punctually and totally. As such, entering into the child's perspective is not self-evident.

This initial focus on the children becomes stronger in the course of the project: *"I should always pay attention to how the children are doing during the activities. I have to make sure they feel at ease and enjoy the activities"*.

The teachers gain more insight into each of the children's levels of involvement and well-being. Already during the class screening, they are inclined to search for the elements which cause the low scores, although they often look for these outside the school setting, for instance with the parents, poverty, lack of material, etc.

Especially the concept of well-being seems to appeal to the teachers and advisors, not only in its function of reflecting on the children: *"Reflecting on well-being touches your inner self. I asked myself how the children were doing, but at the same time I started wondering about my own well-being. It touches me personally."*

(b) Concepts

We find that with the introduction of these concepts, the teachers and advisors give their own – not intended – meaning to them. For example, they interpret well-being as 'welfare' or 'doing well from a materialistic perspective': *"Almost all the Nicaraguan children have a low level of well-being, since they all live in poverty."* However, when someone's level of well-being is low, this can imply that other basic needs apart from the basic material need might remain unfulfilled.

Another example is that they associate involvement with discipline, doing what the teacher asks, finishing the tasks, being punctual and tidy: *"Only a few children in my class do not reach a satisfying level of involvement, most of the children perform their tasks quickly and correctly."* At that stage, they do not realise that involvement is primarily about the child's 'exploratory drive' and 'mental activity'.

They also link competence to 'competition' and in order to find out who is the best, a certain teacher even organised competitions in class. Assessing the level of competence is the most difficult part: the teachers do not seem to grasp the concept of 'average' which is why they do not succeed in assessing the children's level of performance.

One thing is certain, initially many teachers have difficulties in gaining insight in the meaning of the concepts and their respective signals, which can sometimes lead to inaccurate reasoning; for instance *"Luis always participates, which means he feels good"*. One teacher explicitly indicated her confusion, although at the same time she showed that she grasps the essence of both concepts; *"All these signals make my head spin, but what I do know is that well-being involves emotions, being happy or sad, and involvement has to do with participating and learning."* Teachers who do not grasp this essence, often mark the children's scores 'mechanically', for instance by counting the number of positive and negative signals.

Exactly the practice-oriented support sessions provide us with the opportunity to detect these personal interpretations and gradually redirect and sharpen the concepts. During these sessions it also becomes clear that the teachers often succeed in detecting children with extreme low scores for one or both concepts, with or without the (correct) usage of our introduced terminology.

(c) Forms

The advisors should keep in mind that teachers sometimes hesitate to give children a low score. There is a clear tendency to give high scores, while this does not correspond with the picture we have from our own observations. Teachers often consider a low score as a sign of their own failing and fear that this will make a bad impression with their superiors. It is necessary to pay a lot of attention to the true function of the AR-cycle, i.e. as an instrument for self-evaluation and not for control or sanction.

Observations are only a starting point for actions aimed at improvement. In our own supportive relationship with the teachers we succeed in convincing them of the importance to give a score that is true to reality: *"There is no point in fooling myself. Reality is reality and that will not change by marking a higher score on paper"*. Many teachers revise the scores they initially marked (too) high.

It is clear that this issue needs special attention in the Nicaraguan context, where the (quality of the) relationship between the teacher and its advisor, but also between the teacher and the school board and the teacher and the inspection plays an important part. Who has access to which forms, under which conditions and with which intentions?

In the training sessions for the advisors it appears useful to explicitly deal with their role as a partner of the teacher: s/he supports, helps, guides, facilitates, etc. He/she needs to establish the support in a 'context-sensitive' manner, taking into account what is (not yet) possible and needed at that particular moment in that school, with that principle and that teacher.

The advisors in our group indicate that the forms help them to feel more secure about their observations. The instructions and forms help them to determine the focus of their observations and create order in a reality which is sometimes very chaotic to them: *"I used to start observing without knowing what to focus on or what to write down. I just sat there and watched and often did not know what to think. The forms have made me feel more confident and provide me with a more solid foundation."*

4.2 Stage 2: From analysis to targets for actions

After the first phase of the AR-cycle, the teacher has marked down all the children's scores for well-being and involvement. The second stage of the cycle stimulates the teacher to digest and analyse the observations made. Most of the time, this implies collecting new information which will help to gain more insight in the (low) scores and their causes. Gaining a clear picture of the factors which lead to the scores will help the teacher a great deal to find out what it is she needs to work on in order to improve the situation.

Stage 2 starts with filling in form 3: 'Stage 2 - Conclusions Class Screening' where the teacher will first incorporate the screening information in a concise way. The impressions and conclusions resulting from this can steer her in two possible directions: form 4 or form 5.

Form 4: 'Stage 2 – General Approach: Analysis and Targets for Actions' leads her to first route of the cycle which is entirely dedicated to tracing and dealing with the factors in the 'general approach' which cause low scores for a large part of the group. As problems of individual children are sometimes caused by the general educational context and in that case, it is not really efficient to analyse each child individually. The advantage of general measures is that they will benefit the whole group in one way or another. However, for some children these general measures are insufficient, because their problem needs specific interventions. When the teacher wishes to help children individually, she can use form 5: 'Stage 2 – Individual File: Analysis and Targets for Actions'. This will guide her through second route of the cycle, the 'specific approach'.

In the following paragraphs, we will focus on each of the aforementioned forms 3, 4 and 5, describing the experiences of the people who used them.[1]

4.2.1 FORM 3: CONCLUSIONS CLASS SCREENING

First, the teacher fills in the information from stage 1 of the AR-cycle in an overview table. There is room provided for each child's name in one of the 9 cells, formed by the intersection of the two dimensions involvement and competence and the three levels (low, moderate and high) in the top left corner. In addition, the names of the children with a low score for well-being are underlined in red, as demonstrated below:

Table 2: Form 3: combination square: conclusions class screening

C \ B	LOW	AVERAGE	HIGH
LOW			
AVERAGE			
HIGH			

C= competence, B = involvement

Thus, the situation is visualised and gives the teacher at once a clear idea of how her group and each of the children are doing. The same form 3 invites the teacher to put into words the impression s/he gets from this overview by means

---

[1] With regard to the chronology of the project activities, we invited the teachers and advisors to directly tackle stage 3 of the AR-cycle in order to prepare, implement and evaluate concrete initiatives by means of forms 6 and 7, after the analysis of the general approach with form 4. Only then we dealt with form 5 for the analysis of the problems of individual children, again followed by stage 3 in order to tackle form 6 and 7 and take actions to improve the children's situation. However, in this article we respect the order of the stages according to the AR-cycle. After the paragraph on form 4 (general approach) we first take a look at form 5 (individual children) in the next paragraph, before describing the concrete actions for both tracks in stage 3.

of writing down a number of conclusions or aspects which need extra attention relating to the general class setting on the one hand (first route) and the individual children on the other hand (second route). The teacher can indicate her intention to open an individual file for the children whom she is particularly concerned about.

(a) General impact

Stimulating the teachers to work with the information they gathered during the first stage adds to a more child-oriented focus. Again they need to observe each individual child in order to be able to put it in the right box of the table. The teachers call this overview table the 'radiography' of the group. While completing this table with the information on each child, they start seeing an overall picture of how their group and each of the children are doing in the setting. The teachers now talk about the children (with problems) in terms of (the signals of) well-being, involvement and competence.

(b) Concepts

This visualisation clearly reveals score patterns which sometimes indicate that some teachers do not yet sufficiently master the concepts. For example, they mark a high score for competence for the majority of the children, which is not logical when you look at the definitions of the levels. The fact that the teachers are reluctant to mark a low score is a possible cause (see previously), but we believe that they still find it difficult to understand that the levels of competence are obtained by situating the child versus the class 'average'. Another finding is that some teachers very often mark the same levels for involvement and competence in one child. For example, when they mark a high level of competence, they automatically mark a high level of involvement as well. In this case, the overview table with the children's names shows a diagonal line from the top left to the bottom right. This pattern could of course refer to reality, i.e. that the class practice is not tuned in to the children with a low level of competence, which would explain why they automatically have a low level of involvement as well. However, based on our discussions and our own observations, we assume that these teachers have not yet obtained a differentiated picture of the children: they are either doing well or doing badly in every area. They fail to notice that the children's perceptions can vary according to different dimensions, for example, 'feeling at ease, but lacking concentration when participating'.

The support sessions are also extremely valuable with regard to these score patterns: we detect (possible) misconceptions and use them to clarify or even simplify the concepts. For example, with regard to the level of competence, we decide not to ask the teachers anymore to situate the child versus the class average, but versus the class majority. An important source for (possible) rectifications are the teachers themselves, whom we invite to describe children to their colleagues and clarify the marked scores. As such, it becomes clear that for example children with a low level of competence are not per definition unhappy and can even have a high score for involvement. Even the teachers who have gained more insight in the concepts still revise their scores of the first stage.

(c) Form

For some teachers and their advisors it is not evident to manage the more-dimensional overview table. At first, they have difficulties situating the children in the correct box, for example the box that links low involvement to a moderate level of competence. Hence, the necessary to explain a number of examples step by step.

We get the impression that some teachers do not know what the result of the radiography implies. The conclusions they formulate in terms of positive or negative items are rather insignificant and lack empathy. For example, *"I am pleased because most of the children have a high score for involvement. I am dissatisfied because some children have a low level of involvement."*

The advisors are generally enthusiastic about this form of the AR-cycle. One teacher communicates this in terms of the essence of the view on the quality of education and inclusion which we introduce: *"Thanks to the overview table in form 3, you can very easily detect the children who have problems, which are not automatically the handicapped children. One of the teachers whom I sup-port succeeds very well in tuning in the activities to Kenia's capabilities. She had a low level of competence, but a high level of involvement. Kenia's name was not underlined in red, because although she is handicapped, she is not unhappy".*

4.2.2 FORM 4: GENERAL APPROACH - ANALYSIS AND TARGETS FOR ACTION

Form 4 presents a range of aspects and factors which always have an impact on the children's well-being and involvement in one way or another, for example the state of the school building, the size, colours and light in the classrooms, the didactical material and toys, the objectives and contents, the didactical methods, the relations and the teacher's style. It is up to the teacher to investigate and indicate how according to her these factors cause the (low) scores for well-being and involvement. Per aspect or factor the form contains questions which the teacher has to answer by indicating green, orange or red according to whether she is very, moderately or hardly satisfied of the way in which the factor is realized in his/her class practice. Form 4 also provides room for making up an inventory of the targets for action later on, i.e. the factors on which she would like to work in order to improve the children's level of well-being and involvement.

(a) General impact

While the first stage of the AR-cycle focuses on the children, we ask the teachers in this second stage to take a closer look at the (impact of the) educational context. This will make them more conscious of their own share in the recorded (low) scores for well-being and involvement, since they themselves play a considerable part in creating this context. While in the first stage, the teachers spontaneously identified the causes for the low scores outside themselves; in the second stage we gradually see them also identifying the factors within themselves. Especially in the elementary school, this process is far from evident. Here, the process of re-focussing in itself is often cause for resistance. Some teachers feel that they have failed, feel criticised or overwhelmed.

We do not believe that resistance is a phenomenon which should be avoided at all cost in supportive and innovative work. It does not indicate the advisor's failure. On the contrary, it can signal the fact that the advisor has touched a delicate subject with a teacher who 'cares' about her job and about what is linked to it in the supportive sessions. In that case, the resistance originates from 'positive energy', even when this involves the teacher's negative perception. At least, this is how we explain this, when reflecting together with the advisor's on their role as 'innovative agents'. Either way, in the pilot schools this view gives us sufficient inner peace to be receptive to and spend time with the teachers to explore their (negative) perceptions. We find that after the initial resistance, most teachers are willing to master and support the new method of analysis. We want to examine the setting with all its positive and negative aspects in order to discover opportunities for improvement. The range of initiatives the teachers will take later on in stage 3 (see paragraph 4.3 and 5) proves that they share this view.

(b) Concepts

Initially, the meaning of each aspect in form 4 does not fully sink in, certainly not the five didactical factors (atmosphere and relation, tuning in to the child's level, closeness to reality, activity and initiative) and the 3 dimensions of the teacher's style (empathy for the children's perception, stimulating interventions, giving autonomy). The first general screening, which the teachers complete in form 4, seems to function rather as 'an introduction' providing them with a vague picture of what it is about. But in order to help them fully grasp the core of it, various extensive support sessions are necessary, where we analyse various class observations by means of the factors. We continue these analyses in stage 3, but we also encourage the teachers to apply the acquired information in the preparation, implementation and evaluation of their courses and activities.

(c) Forms

The resistance caused by form 4, indicates that initially the teachers do not question their own approach when marking the factors. Again, they are reluctant to mark red (unsatisfying) scores, and when they do mark a red score, they only do so for external factors such as the building, school facilities, the number of pupils and materials.

Moreover, we find that some teachers mark scores which are socially desirable, for example *"I did not mark a red score for the 'state of the school building' and for the 'lack of materials' because it would seem as though I'm criticizing the principle, since he is responsible for these things"* or we find that the teachers do not evaluate the real situation: *"We do not have a lot of didactical materials, which is a real pity. I would like to have more, but compared to other schools, we are doing ok. That is why I marked a green score"*.

The teachers generally mark their own pedagogical-didactical approach (the five factors and teacher's style) green (satisfying). Does this again reflect their fear of making a bad impression with the school board or inspection?

After a while and after having discussed various class observations and analyses, the function of form 4 as a self-evaluation and reflection tool becomes clearer: *"If I mark a green score for all the factors, I am fooling myself"*. Assessing the situation is, again, nothing more than a starting point from which to look for opportunities for improvement. Reassured by this, many teachers start marking more realistic scores, keeping their rubber close at hand. Also factors which refer to their own approach now receive a red score.

The advisors regard form 4 as the core of the AR-cycle. While the first stage still deals with the children, the second focuses entirely on the teachers themselves: *"In my opinion, form 4 is the most important form. It makes the teacher evaluate him/herself. The introduction of this form was rather difficult, since the teacher was afraid to admit mistakes and consequently merely indicated external factors as a cause for problems. For instance, she thought that the cause for her lack of discipline lied in the children, since they were being difficult and hyperactive. But now that she knows she can count on me, she is able to admit her own strengths and weaknesses."*

The advisors regard form 4 as the actual implementation of the broadened view and job description which we wish to introduce. It does not only involve the handicapped child, but also the educational context in which the child is embedded. Improving the general approach will not only benefit one child, but all the children in the group. Form 4 provides the advisors with a basic foundation to implement this broadened focus. It helps them to structure the observations and document their conversations with the teachers.

4.2.3 FORM 5: INDIVIDUAL FILE - ANALYSIS AND TARGETS FOR ACTION

When in form 4 the teacher expresses the intention to open an individual file for a particular child, she actually intents to fill in form 5 for this child. In the first place, this should help her to understand how the child is functioning before embarking on seeking solutions. Apart from general information (why do I open this file, what is my impression of the child, what about the home setting), the teacher will also fill in more specific information about the child's well-being in various relational fields (classmates, teacher, class and school setting, family members) and the child's involvement and competence in various situations, activities and subjects. When making up the balance afterwards, the teacher will also explicitly take into account the positive aspects and strengths of the child and its situation, in order to come to solutions. Formulating targets for action is the first step in finding these solutions.

(a) General impact

When embarking on the introduction of this form, the school year is almost over. Only in October the teachers get around to opening an individual file for the child they were concerned about in form 3 already in April or May. Once the teachers have become more familiar with the AR-cycle, it will not take that long. They will be able to analyse the general approach by means of form 4, while at the same time opening an individual file for one or several children by means of form 5. However, the teachers have now obtained a general idea of how this all works. They notice how the same parameters are used, which form a thread throughout the AR-cycle: well-being and involvement. This once again highlights the essence of our broad view on inclusion: the teacher only opens a file for children who have a problem, which are not necessarily handicapped children. As such, the teachers gain insight into the situation of at lease one child in the group, for whom they come up with and implement concrete actions in stage 3.

(b) Concepts

A number of terms in the form need some clarification or simplification. The teachers have difficulties understanding concepts like empathy, self-organisation, the difference between social competence and social attitude; a whole new ground to be developed in the future. For example the exploration of the 'empathic basic attitude' and its implementation by means of the experiential dialogue is an extremely interesting domain, waiting to be explored. Numerous class observations and discussions will probably be necessary to gradually grasp the essence of each of these concepts.

(c) Form

The fact that we introduce so many (new) terms seems to confuse a number of teachers and advisors. Moreover, some get lost in the numerous sections and sub-sections of the form: *"Where do I fill in which piece of information?"*. We asked ourselves whether we shouldn't, for the time being, limit ourselves to the most essential part, even if this would mean not being complete? However, users have told us that although the form is very extensive and takes a lot of time to complete, not one single element is superfluous. Together with the advisors we learn that it is often better to first let the teachers tell their story about the child before writing down the elements in a more structured and complete way.

It is clear that the teachers still need close support in order to use the form correctly, both for the technical aspects (what do the sections and concepts mean, where do I fill in which pieces of information, etc) and the contents. Essentially, form 5 steers the teacher to a reconstruction of the child's experiences. In order to learn this, the teachers need extra support and guidance.

Either way, this form proves to be a helpful instrument in the future. The teachers react in a positive way: *"This form helps us to reflect on the child and it makes it a lot easier for us to find what we should do to help the child"*. The fact that we clearly emphasise the importance of gaining insight into the positive aspects and strengths of the child and its environment, seems to help them as well: *"Thanks to form 5, I gained more insight in the child's positive and negative aspects. The child is no longer a problem child. We used to label the children according to their problems, but we now realise that the child's strengths are also important, since they can help us to find strategies to improve their situation."* Another positive aspect is the fact that the teachers' interest for the children's home setting increases. In some cases, the reflection and action work

161

done by the teachers even strengthens the relation between the school and family setting.

4.3 Stage 3: From targets for action to interventions

The analyses of the former stage create an overall picture of what causes the recorded (low) scores for well-being and involvement. This results in the formulation of a number of targets for action, which still remain general for the time being. Based on this, the teacher can now start working on his/her class practice in order to improve the situation, either of the entire class via general interventions which benefit all the children (first route of the AR-cycle), or of one or a few children for whom specific interventions are necessary because of the seriousness of their individual problems (second route).

Form 6: 'Stage 3 - Interventions: Planning' supports the teacher in coming up with actions. It stimulates him/her to concretise what it is s/he wants to achieve (goals) and clearly set out and plan the steps s/he has to take to get there (action points).
Form 7: 'Stage 3 - Interventions: Reporting' is meant as a tool which helps the teacher to look back at the implemented actions: have the goals been reached with a positive effect on the children's involvement and well-being?
This instance of self-evaluation makes the AR-cycle complete: from observing how the children are doing, to analysing the factors which have an impact on this, to planning actions in order to improve the situation, to evaluating the actions: is there actual improvement?

(a) General impact

When working according to this reflection, planning, action and evaluation pattern, the teachers take numerous initiatives. Following are some examples of general interventions (first route). They relate to 3 of the 5 didactical factors, since we decided to concentrate on these (see 'concepts').

• General interventions in nursery school:

Factor *'Activity'*:
- Avoid long waiting periods before the children can start the activity, by organising not one but several movement activities at the same time in the playground (five-year-olds).
- Invite the children to distribute the materials themselves during manual activities (five-year-olds).

Factor *'Closeness to Reality'*:
- Change the pattern of first having to talk about something (e.g. growth of a bean plant) and only afterwards experiencing or doing it concretely (e.g. sowing the seeds of a bean).
- Change the pattern of teaching about 'isolated, elements lacking context' (e.g. the colour brown) to meaningful total activities (e.g. observing the plants in the school garden, planting new plants and observing them in all their aspects, not only their colour) (five-year-olds).

For other activities we refer to paragraph 5: 'Stimulating a Different Approach in Nursery School: Playing is Learning'.

• General Interventions in Elementary School:

Factor *'Tuning in to the Child's Level'*:
- Differentiation during language and arithmetic lessons by means of instructions and exercises tuned in to the children with a low level of competence and involvement (first year).

Factor *'Activity'*:
- Arithmetic instruction cards which the children can do in pairs (first year).
- Repetition of the multiplication tables by means of a hopscotch diagram (third year).

Factor *'Closeness to Reality'* and *'Activity'*:
- Each of the pupils creates his/her own ecosystem in a bottle (fifth year).

Following are examples of specific interventions aimed at individual children (second route). These are still mainly formulated in terms of 'targets for action' instead of concretised 'action points'. This is simply because this year we have made less progress as expected with regard to the second route (as we already mentioned before).

- Improving the relationship between teacher and child (e.g. try to get closer to the child, start a conversation, give a cuddle,…).
- Improving the child's relationship with the other children (e.g. invite the child to distribute materials, pay the child a compliment,...).
- Tuning in the activities to the child's level and interests.
- Not forcing the child to come in front of the classroom and make exercises which are too difficult, resulting in total failure.
- Hygiene, e.g. giving the child a wash, delousing the child, etc.
- Involving the parents for example via conversations at the school gate.

(b) Concepts

The aforementioned initiatives seem obvious, but coming up with and implementing them is not at all evident for most of the teachers in the Nicaraguan context. The initiatives are often preceded by numerous supportive discussions. As such, what we invite them to do should not be underestimated: questioning the widespread and so familiar approach which they often have been implementing for years and with which they themselves have grown up when they went to school as a child. At the same time, we ask them to use all their intellectual capacities and pedagogical-didactical skills.

Already during stage 2 of the AR-cycle we experienced that the analysis of the general class setting via form 4 was too general to offer the teachers sufficient support in formulating targets for action and concrete action points. Hence the necessity to start from concretely observed lessons or activities which we can then analyse together with the teachers by means of the involvement factors. At that stage, most of the teachers will not yet succeed in doing the analysis autonomously. Most of the time we start presenting and analysing our own observations. Through the conversations arising from this, most of the teachers really start to comprehend what a certain factor entails and what working on that factor really means. In order to facilitate the reflection and action, we decide after a while to concentrate on only three factors, which we find are most essential and at the same time most problematic in the given situation, namely 'tuning in to the child's level', 'activity' and 'closeness to reality'.

With regard to these targets for action, form 4 of the AR-cycle merely suggests in which direction one should orientate the focus on improvement. When the teacher marks the factor 'tuning in to the child's level' red, she acknowledges the fact that she realises that this aspect needs improvement. The AR-cycle however does not provide her with concrete information on 'how' she can improve that aspect. It is up to the teacher's and advisor's own creativity to come up with alternative approaches. It would be helpful, if they could use some kind of model suggesting in which direction they should orientate their concrete initiatives, in other words a practical guide with practical assignments, instructions, suggestions, implementation schemes, etc. which one could con- sult apart from the AR-cycle in order to work on each of the factors.

(c) Forms

The teachers plan the actions together with the advisor, for whom this constitutes again an extension of his/her task. The advisor does not only set up an implementation plan for the handicapped child –like before- but s/he now also observes the general class setting and the children embedded in it, together with the teacher in order to come up with improvements.

The advisors regard the forms as an invaluable support in helping them to implement the analysis and action in a structured way together with the teacher: *"I used to come up with solutions right away, which the teacher then had to implement. Now, I first observe, then sit together with the teacher to analyse the problem and only then we look for solutions."*
By going through this process together, the chance of actual implementation and success of the actions appears to increase. Moreover, form 7 clearly states that the work is not limited to planning actions. The teacher and advisor should do a close follow-up and monitoring. Again this is a new aspect which draws the advisors' attention: *"My job used to be limited to making* suggestions *and I did not really check whether they were monitored afterwards. I did however notice that most of them were not really monitored. Whereas now, I first discuss things with the teacher in order to come to an agreement together. Afterwards, I evaluate the implementation and results together with the teacher. Following the form's guidelines, we plan the dates of the actions beforehand, which provides me with a good framework."*

5 Stimulating a different approach in nursery school: playing is learning

Specifically in the nursery school the reflection steers us to questioning the basic approach of class practice itself. The supportive work in nursery school leads us to extremely interesting findings with regard to the improvement of the basic class practice.

We start reflecting on the basic approach of class practice when it becomes clear that the children during their half hour of 'free initiative' ('libre opción') reach far higher scores for involvement than during compulsory class activities guided by the teacher.
When bringing this up, we find out that the teachers themselves feel rather uncomfortable with the basic approach as well. One teacher remarks: *"It is as if I'm working with pupils in elementary school. I have to force them in order to keep them involved in the activities. It should not be this way"*. Someone says: *"Only during free play, the children seem to get started. It's as if they have been waiting for it"*. And also the following remark clearly shows that the teachers do not feel at ease with the basic approach: *"Sometimes, the children are enthusiastically telling me what they have experienced. For example a*

165

terrible accident in which a pregnant woman died. The children asked me what happened with the baby. I explained to them that the woman carried the baby in her belly, like a kangaroo, but then completely inside her belly. But the curriculum limits us in these kinds of discussions, although themes like this are often tackled by the children and really appeal to them. But if the inspector would enter the classroom at that moment, he would accuse me of improvising.

The teachers themselves do not spontaneously come to the conclusion that broadening free initiative could be a valuable alternative for their present class practice. They do not see the true value of this free moment of choice. They let the children play and watch them from a distance. For them as well as for the children this means nothing more than a welcome break between two guided activities. This becomes clear by means of one of the teachers' apologetic remarks, when we enter her classroom for observation: "*Sorry, but the guided activity's already finished. It is now free play, the children are just playing* ".
Initially, the teachers find it strange when we specifically want to focus on free initiative during a set of four team meetings. Our intention is to make the teachers familiar with the invaluable meaning of an 'open learning environment' where the children can learn and develop; to help them to create the right conditions (areas, materials, impulses) and to gradually guide the way to broadening free pupil initiative and limiting the number of closely guided compulsory class activities.
We keep our focus on the closely guided curriculum-oriented activities and stimulate the teachers to keep on improving them. But additionally, we open a second supportive route for free initiative. This certainly strengthens the reflections work and results in a whole range of new initiatives.

We dedicate the following team meetings to four action points (AP):
• re-arranging the classroom into different areas
• increasing the materials on offer
• stimulating interventions
• broadening free initiative

AP1: Re-arranging the classroom into different areas

We invite the teachers to make an inventory of the existing areas and materials in the classroom and ask them to create at least one new area. The teachers start taking initiatives and create for example a music area, a sports area or a medical area.
We decide to limit the number of 'decorating and watch areas' and increase the number of 'do and action areas' where the children can actively play.

Furthermore, the classrooms are still too open with a table and chair for every child. We would like to see more separations between the different areas. An important step is taking away the superfluous chairs and tables, but the school board and the teachers find this very drastic, since they have just made a great financial effort in order to give each child a table and chair. Moreover, they will have to justify towards the parents why their children are not 'learning' at a table anymore but are 'playing' on the floor.

AP 2: Increasing materials on offer

A constant concern of the teachers is the lack of materials and the financial means to obtain them. We decided to use our imagination and create an inventory of all the desired materials and strategies to obtain them.

Naturally, it is impossible to obtain every single item on that list, but the teachers do succeed in increasing the materials on offer significantly:

- A lot of re-usable materials collected by the teachers and parents at home;
- A number of real-life objects such as clothing, irons, a telephone, an alarm clock, etc. from parents, neighbours or family;
- A dozen of big boxes full of wooden blocks and small boards obtained from a parent carpenter;
- The creation of a water and sand basin in the playground by the school board with the profit of the school shop.

Although the teachers did not succeed in obtaining every single item on the list, they now realise that new materials not necessarily cost fortunes. An important 'side effect' is that the parents feel more involved in their children's school life. Also due to the enthusiastic reactions of the children, increasing the materials on offer has now become a permanent point of attention for the teachers. But the most important effect of this action point might well be that the teachers feel that they themselves are able to improve things in their own class practice. This is invaluable, since they used to work with the feeling that they themselves were not able to change the situation and that they depended on the help of others. In the future, we plan team meetings on how to make play/learning materials like puzzles, loto's, domino's, abacuses etc.

AP 3: Stimulating interventions

Enriching the setting with new areas and materials means creating good material conditions. Whether this enables the children to learn and develop mostly depends on the teachers' role as 'mediator', a role that they at that moment do not yet master. They do not really see the value of play and interpret 'free play' literally, as 'not interfering' or 'letting the children be'. Reason enough for us to do something about this.

167

In order to teach the teachers how to observe opportunities to learn and develop during free play, we invite them to play like children and build a bridge with the materials on offer. This convinces them of the value of free play. It offers a great deal of learning opportunities in various developmental areas. Moreover, it reassures them that these are also part of the official curriculum, on which they focus during closely guided class activities. If the children can learn the same things in free play, why would you still organise these compulsory activities that do not appeal to the children? This is the message we try to get across. It should indicate that playing is not a break, but a valuable activity which can be even more valuable when the teachers take up their role as a true mentor instead of retreating. In order to orientate them towards this role, we focus together on the (quality of the) interactions between teacher and child. Key question of the reflection is: what can we do to stimulate learning during free play? (experiential dialogue, interventions, communication and stimulation of reflection, open questions, etc.) As a starting point we take the teachers' own interactions and invite them to write them down on a piece of paper and screen them together on their stimulating quality.

In the future, we want to keep on improving the teachers' observation and stimulation skills. First, we invite them to implement what they have learnt when the children are playing in the sand and water basins in the playground. This will also convince the school board that the financial investment in the sand and water basins actually was an investment in the children's learning and development.

AP 4: Broadening free initiative

Until now, the teachers have not yet broadened free initiative in their class practice. They are not ready for this yet, since we are still preparing them to take that step. They still cling to the official daily routine with one or two instances of free play, although some tend to limit the guided activities and extend free play. The foundation has been established, yet still needs strengthening in the future. Since this change is so drastic, discussion and co-ordination with the regional and national authorities are absolutely necessary.

6 Reflections

6.1 Experiential Education as frame of reference

One year of effective practical work in the schools, together with the teachers and their advisors, convinces us that the EXE framework functions well within the Nicaraguan context. The concepts of well-being and involvement clearly refer to a reality which also prevails in the Nicaraguan educational context: there are children who are to a high or low extent (mentally) active during activities and children who feel happy or who have emotional difficulties. Simply identifying and naming this recognisable reality by means of a frame of concepts, appears to be an important step in the learning process of the teachers and their advisors.

The EXE framework situates the above-mentioned process variables versus a set of approach and context variables on the one hand and the success of education on the other hand. As such, order is created in what many teachers and advisors experience as chaos. By differentiating all elements and linking them to each other, the EXE frame offers an invaluable foundation to untangle reality. The frame of concepts helps them to make an overall picture and understand what is going on in the group and how the factors have an impact on the school and class setting. It facilitates reflection, which brings all elements back to that final touchstone of the quality of education, i.e. the children's well-being and involvement.

Both orientation points allow a broadening of inclusion and direct the attention to all children who are in one way or another at risk within the actual educational context and approach. Hence, working on inclusion means working on the general quality of education with special attention for children with special educational needs.

6.2 Implementation

We can conclude that well-being and involvement are also an educational reality in Nicaragua. However, one cannot expect the teachers and advisors to master the full meaning of these concepts at once. No, being able to observe children through these 'glasses of quality' is part of the process itself. Based on what the teachers and advisors told us during the supportive discussions and various practical assignments, we can conclude that it is necessary to clarify and refine these concepts. Naturally, this applies to all EXE-concepts introduced by the AR-cycle and to the entire educational philosophy behind it.

Is the AR-cycle the most appropriate instrument to steer this process of learning and innovation? Forms 1, 2 and 3 have proved their value in orientating the teachers' focus towards the children.

When introducing form 4 (Screening the General Approach), it merely functions as a first encounter with the entirety of the approach or context factors. But colouring these factors according to the codes of satisfaction already requires a certain amount of insight. But the step from this to determining targets for action and concrete initiatives has been proven too big for most teachers. Only by presenting a whole range of concrete analyses of observed classes and activities can the teachers grasp the true meaning of the factors and can they observe how their basic class practice is doing in order to come to accurate targets for action. In order to offer the teachers and their advisors some more inspiration to help them to come up with concrete actions, they need a practical guide with the possible implementations. The second support circuit in nursery school convinces us of the necessity of this. We can conclude that the teachers are able to implement very useful actions with regard to re-arranging the classroom, stimulating interventions, etc by means of our suggestions.

6.3 Conclusion

We would like to gain some more practical experience with forms 6 and 7 in order to be able to draw a number of final conclusions with regard to their function and possible changes. This also applies to form 5, although its essence should certainly be preserved.

On the whole, the introduced pattern of 'gaining insight-analysis-action-evaluation' should be maintained. Certainly because the teachers (and their advisors) tend to skip the analysis and go straight to finding solutions, while it is exactly the analysis which helps them to gain more insight in the situation. Starting from the analysis it is easier to embark on the implementation of goal-oriented improvements which will have a better chance at success.

Probably due to the difficult working and living conditions and the teacher's limited pedagogical-didactical background, the learning and changing process is slow. In order to achieve a fundamental effect, direct, close and continuous support is necessary. It is never wise to introduce a theory to the teachers and send them back to their practice without some kind of monitoring or follow-up. However, this seems often to be the case within the Nicaraguan training practice, possibly due to the very limited financial means. The different types of training activities (continuous courses, workshops and practical support and team meetings in school) have proved to be essential in order to obtain the aforementioned impact results.

Certainly in the context of a developing country it is hopeful to see a lot of potential for future change i.e. didactical methods, relations, teacher's style, etc and this even without big investments in materials (classroom facilities, pedagogical-didactical materials). There are still a lot of 'free' measures that can be taken in these areas, which can make a huge difference in terms of well-being and involvement. The examples we gave of the initiatives taken by the teachers indicate that these are often very simple but extremely effective. Especially the EXE model has proved to be extremely powerful in this regard. One year of effective work in the Nicaraguan schools has certainly been a fruitful and more than promising start to develop the existing potential for change.

References

Laevers, F. & Van Sanden, P. (1989). *Basisboek voor een ervaringsgerichte kleuterklaspraktijk. Reeks kleuteronderwijs nr. 1.* Leuven: Centrum voor Ervaringsgericht Onderwijs.

Laevers, F., (1992). *Ervaringsgericht werken in de basisschool. Reeks Basisonderwijs nr. 1.* Leuven: Centrum voor Ervaringsgericht Onderwijs.

Laevers, F. (1998). *Een procesgericht kindvolgsysteem voor leerlingen. Handleiding en formulierenset. Reeks Basisonderwijs nr. 3.* Leuven: Centrum voor Ervaringsgericht Onderwijs.

Laevers, F. (Red.) (2001). *Procesgericht kindvolgsysteem voor kleuters. Achtergrond en praktijksuggesties.* Leuven: Centrum voor Ervaringsgericht Onderwijs.

Van Sanden, P. & Joly, A., (Red.) (2000). *Módulo básico: un ciclo de reflexion y accion sobre el bienestar y el involucramiento como pautas en la educacion inclusiva* [onuitgegeven versie].

UNESCO, UNICEF, MECD/BID (2001). *Plan nacional de educacion 2001-2015.*

A PROCESS-ORIENTED SELF-ASSESSMENT INSTRUMENT FOR STUDENTS IN TEACHER TRAINING
Ludo Heylen

1 Situation in teacher training in Flanders

Teacher training for teachers in pre-school, primary and secondary education (age 12-15) is organised in teacher training colleges. It is a post-secondary course of three years in non-university higher education. From the beginning of the course the training is focused on the field of action: students in the section of pre-school teachers learn to know the pre-school, students preparing for primary are from the beginning oriented to the primary school. There are not much common activities between the different courses.

For many years the teacher training colleges were working on a rather traditional base. In the past these colleges were linked with a secondary school and the way of teaching was not adjusted for Higher education. The last ten or fifteen years, since the innovation of higher education, teacher training colleges are searching for an own identity. We can see initiatives for new approaches: modules being introduced, problem based learning,... The problem is that there is no clear structure or vision in most of these initiatives. Too often a lot of new ideas were brought together without any cohesion.

Together with the search for new approaches there is a need for more information about the possibilities within the new culture of assessment in higher education. Ideas of co-assessment, peer-assessment, self-assessment, overall exams, assessment-centres are recently dominating discussions in teacher training often without structured initiatives.

Although the content in many teacher training colleges changes and most of these colleges choose for a child-centred approach in elementary school (for which these students are trained), the approach in the colleges are not yet student-centred. This means that there is a gap between the explicit vision of the trainers and the implicit actions. They want to teach students to be child-centred by telling them to keep in touch with the feelings of the children, to listen to them, to start from their interests... but in the way they introduce these topics they are too much teacher-centred instead of student-centred. In this situation the impact of the story is not what you can expect of it because the influence of the implicit ideas seems to be more powerful. The principle of 'teach what you preach' is not respected.

A lot of students don't make the transfer to the second year. There is a high percentage of drop-out. More than 50% doesn't succeed in reaching the second year. Probably too many students have not the right expectations when they start the studies. They don't know exactly which capacities they need to be successful. Some of them are coming from vocational studies in secondary and are not well prepared for starting higher education; others are coming from disadvantaged backgrounds or ethnic minorities and don't feel at ease in teacher training. This means that in the first year of teacher training a lot of -not successful- energy is going to a group of students who will drop out after the first year. This is also for the trainers a demoralising experience.

Within this situation we can see that there are no coloured teachers in the pre- or primary schools in Flanders (a few in secondary); although in many elementary schools in cities more than 50% of the learners is from an ethnic minority group. This is a topic that needs our special attention.

2 Aims of the process-oriented self-assessment instrument

Within this context a self-assessment instrument was developed in order to create a possibility to answer a lot of the problems we mentioned above. The instrument aims to realise two objectives.

Enhance the changes in teacher training for all students and especially the students that are in danger for dropping out.

With the instrument we want to improve the opportunities for students to succeed in the colleges. This means that the students should be aware of how they are doing, should be aware of possible problems, should see opportunities to solve their problems... A first step in this process is that the student needs to make a roundup of how she/he is functioning in the learning environment. This process-oriented self-assessment instrument offers the items to guide her/him. By completing the different forms the student is invited to give answers to fund-amental questions about her/his well-being and involvement in the different courses of the colleges. The scores of the instrument can give students and counsellors direction for concrete remedial actions.

Create a teacher training practise based on a student-centred approach.

The scores based on this self-assessment instrument can also help curriculum developers to create a new pedagogical approach. By looking at the levels of involvement students give them very valuable feedback. Involvement is the indicator to measure the quality of what is being offered in the training.

Starting from this information, an approach with more attendance to skills and competencies instead of mere contents can be developed. In line with the ideas of 'active learning' they can make work of the principle 'teach what you preach' by involving the students more in the process of learning.

3 The instrument SMS-EXE

3.1 Developing the instrument

We started by developing a questionnaire with 6 different forms asking for :

- an overview of well-being, involvement, interest, competence and approach for all courses. (1)
- well-being in the teacher training college (general) (2)
- well-being in a specific course (repeated for each course) (3)
- involvement in a specific course (repeated for each course) (4)
- well-being during ones own teaching practise (5)
- involvement during ones own teaching practise (6)

The questionnaire is based on the theory of 'Experiential Education' and especially on the process-oriented child monitoring system that had been developed for preschool, for primary education and for secondary education. Starting with a clear vision on quality of education makes it easier to make the right conclusions afterwards. In other instruments we often could see a mix of different ideas and especially for interventions afterwards this is creating problems.

The questionnaire was offered in groups of lecturers and students separately in 3 different teacher training institutes. They gave us feedback for changes in the forms.
Also from a colleague in New-Zealand we got a lot of help for constructing the forms. She was willing to introduce the instrument with her students.

The instrument is more than just completing the forms. The collected data represent a firm basis to define goals for further action in the perspective of the improvement of the quality of the training. The findings can be used to see which students need our special attention in order to enhance their development in teacher training. That's why we start calling the system a Student Monitoring System (SMS-EXE) based on Experiential Education.

3.2 A five point scale

In 'form 1' the students assess five different topics for each of the courses or subject matters.

They give on a five point scale a score for these five topics. Score 1 is a very low level of well-being or involvement. Level 5 is the highest level.

- Well-being. *"To what extent do I feel good when participating in this course?"*
- Involvement. *"To what extent do I feel engaged when participating in this course?"*
- Interest. *"To what extent am I interested in this course?"*
- Competence. *"To what extent do I feel competent in this course?"*
- My approach. *"To what extent do I manage to organise myself in relation to this course?"*

For each topic there are subitems to look at. For example:
What does affect my involvement?
✓ I find that this activity matches my level of competence
✓ I find that this subject makes sense and is useful
✓ I am stimulated to be (mentally) active
✓ I am given the space to take initiative in this course

3.4 Two routes

After completing the form two different routes will be followed: an individual track and a track for the group as a whole.

The questions within the individual route are: What is my commitment in this teacher training? Which are my strenghts? Which are my weaknesses? This can lead to assistance in analysing the individual results, in students counselling, in guidance with subject matter knowledge, in social-emotional assitance.

The questions within the track of the group results are: What are the results of the group? Which are the strenghts in this course/college? Which are the weaknesses in this course/college?

This can lead to further data-collection and analysis of data, in a need for a general approach, in a search for new didactical approaches, in a search for new ways to organise the teacher training practise.

3.4 Introduction of the instrument

Not all forms have to be completed. The college can choose to introduce only one form or several forms. Form 1 brings an overview of all different courses in the college. Form 3 and 4 are offering more items about well-being (3) and involvement (4) in one course and form 5 and 6 are referring to the teacher training practise. Form 2 is questioning the well-being in the college in general. All forms are related to each other. Most Teacher Training Colleges started by introducing form 2.

We have followed a shame for introducing the SMS-EXE in the different settings of the action-research (table 1).

Table 1: Steps within the SMS-EXE

Step 1: Introducing the SMS-EXE in the Teacher Training
Introducing the SMS-EXE with the decision-makers of the college ❑ Information about the system ❑ Agreement about using the instrument in the college
Introducing the SMS-EXE with the lecturers ❑ Information about the system ❑ Agreement of all lecturers about the use of the SMS-EXE in the teacher training (with acceptance of the consequences of the system for the curriculum and the support of individual students). ❑ Installing the CD on the computer system of the college.
Introducing the SMS-EXE with the students ❑ Information about the concepts well-being an involvement ❑ Practical information about how to complete the forms on the computer ❑ Installing the student representatives ❑ Information about the possibilities and the use of the system
Creating procedures for assistance and support with the decision-makers ❑ The SMS-EXE is not only a diagnostic instrument but aims also to do something with the collected data. In order to guarantee concrete actions we create procedures for assistance and support for each teacher training college. In these procedures there is clearness about where students can expect support for assistance for content matters or where lectures can ask for support to work on enhancing involvement in the courses.
Step 2 : Completing the forms
Students complete the form(s) on the computer in the college.
All data are collected on a central computer.
Step 3 : Discussion about the collected data
Group scores ❑ Students discuss the group scores by answering in group a small questionnaire. ❑ Meeting with the student representatives and formulating conclusions
Individual scores ❑ Meeting with individuals to find clearness in which problems must be untangled.
Step 4 : Start support and concrete actions
Student counselling ❑ Concrete actions in supporting students in their study work.
Curriculum development ❑ Concrete actions in improving courses of lecturers ❑ Concrete actions in improving the curriculum

4 Action-research

4.1 In small groups

In February 2001 we started with introducing the instrument in small groups. We did it in 10 different groups from 5 to 30 students.
First findings:
- The instrument gives students a guideline for evaluating their own way of functioning in the college
- The instrument shows to be a good tool for starting a discussion about the quality of the college
- Some items should be rewritten because students intend to interpret the items as an evaluation of the lecturers
- Some items could not been interpreted equally by all students and should be adjusted

Based on the findings of this try-out we started editing the items again and created a new version of this self-assessment-instrument. This version was transformed into a digital version. For this digital version we have been writing a manual for students for solving possible problems.

Table 2 : Action-research

Period	Action	Number of teacher training colleges	Number of different studies (Preschool, primary, secondary)	Number of students	Number of groups
Feb. '02 June '02	Small groups	4	3	187	10
Nov. '02 Dec. '02	Larger Groups	2	3	950	37

4.2 Action-research with large groups

In order to start collecting data in larger groups we needed to create a digital system for data management. In November 2001 we could start working in large groups in two different teacher training colleges. We worked with all students from the first and the second year for pre-school, primary and secondary school teachers. In school 1 about 600 students were involved; in school 2 about 350.

The digital version

a) The digital version is still showing a possible obstacle. Especially students from the preschool teacher training are not used to explore the possibilities of the computer technology. For them we have to lower the threshold by creating an easier access to the program. (Maybe there can be some hesitation from students coming from ethnic minorities too although we could not find evidence for this statement).

b) Not all students had completed the instrument, and that is an important signal. We still need to investigate the reasons, but there are some indications. Students have to complete the forms on the college (they can not do it at home by using internet). Often it is an extra time investment. For some groups we came in a very busy period of practise. And especially in those groups the response for completing the form was rather low. Some students doubted the usefulness of completing the forms. Anyway all these problems gives us reason to think that the use of the instruments should be an integrated and essential part of the program. In the try-outs is was too often an instrument that we -as externals- introduced.

c) Some items still need an adjustment because we could not interpret them equally for all students. Especially some sub items in form 1 need our special attention.

d) The digital version gives new possibilities for using the different forms. We are thinking of building links between the different forms. For example when a students is scoring a level 2 on involvement for a course in form 1 there will be an automatic link with form 3. Completing form 3 will gives us more information about what is going on.

Validity individual scores

a) The individual scores give a clear picture of how the student is doing within the courses and offer a handhold for individual interventions. The students are capable to assess themselves by completing the form and the items show to be valid for the purpose of student counselling.

b) Students are capable to use involvement and well-being as quality indicators for their own learning. They can see the importance of this approach for their future professional behaviour and they find it evident that these quality indicators are central in their own teacher training college.

179

c) The use of the instrument gives us indication of consequential validity[1]. It means that the assessment brought the consequences we wanted. We have indications for the fact that completing the form gives students insights by getting aware of what and how they are doing in the college. The self-assessment on a regular base gives them ideas to handle their study problems more successfully.

Group scores

a) The group scores give a clear picture of what is running smoothly in the training and what needs to be changed. It offers ideas for interventions on the level of a general approach.
b) In the discussion students seem to be experts in analysing the pedagogical situation in the different courses. They can indicate exactly where problems started and what should be done to solve them.
c) Students are in general very loyal to the lecturers of the college and are very discreet in giving critical remarks.
d) The group scores give students the possibility to discuss in an open atmosphere things that can be improved in the teacher training. The SMS-EXE is giving students a voice in the decision making.
e) The use of the instrument gives us indications of consequential validity. We have indication for the fact that the group scores make lecturers think about what they are doing and how they are offering classes. The SMS-EXE is a crucial instrument in changing the curriculum to a student-centred approach.

Example

Workload is a topic of discussion in higher education. In the forms we don't ask questions about the workload for students and maybe this sounds very strange. But what we do is asking questions in the forms about the students well-being in relation to the courses. Only when we see that there is a problem with well-being we will continue by asking students to identify the reasons for that low level of well-being. It is only at that stage that workload can pop up as

---

[1] Within the new assessment culture the new edumetric approach is giving four crucial criteria for quality of the assessments (Dochy, Heylen, Van de Mosselaer 2002):
- The validity of the task. The task to be done by the students needs to be a reflection of the construct, the skills we want to measure. The thinking skills must be the same thinking skills experts use in their profession.
- The validity (and reliability) of the evaluation. This means that we must be explicit in using the right criteria for evaluation.
- Generalization of the assessment
- The consequencial validity

a determining factor. A student told us that this is the right way to do. He told that, yes, the workload is to heavy but in general he is feeling very happy in the program of the college. And indeed the first question you should ask is about this general feeling and not about workload.

5 The SMS-EXE and other student monitoring systems

The SMS-EXE has something typical that we can not find in other monitoring systems. We give an overview of the most important differences.

- the SMS-EXE starts by making students aware of the situation they are in *by self-assessment*. The items are confronting. This is a crucial factor in helping students with student advice because the first step in student support is getting aware of what is going on.
- the SMS-EXE is not only focusing on the diagnosis of the problems but is putting a lot of effort in helping students by *analysing the results and asking the right questions* for assistance. Often we could see that asking the 'right' question for support is a difficult threshold to take.
- the SMS-EXE is focusing on *Well-being and Involvement*. Especially for the consequential validity this is crucial.
- the SMS-EXE is creating *specific procedures* to work on the detected problems.
- the SMS-EXE provides information for student counselling *and* curriculum improvement.

6 The future

The SMS-EXE is a self assessment instrument that gives a global overview of how students experience the training. Within the instrument there are links to competences and skills. With another self-assessment instrument (DP-EXE) we want to focus on the competences and skills a future teacher need to develop to become an 'experiential teacher'. Both instruments will be crucial in realising a student-centred education. It will influence the way teacher training is dealing with curriculum development and the organisation of the courses.

Not only teacher training departments are showing interest in the instrument, also other departments at the level of higher education want to know more about the SMS-EXE. In the future we hope to do more action research in different departments in order to increase the validity of our instruments with the new findings.

7 Conclusions

With this SMS-EXE we have a powerful instrument to get a clear picture of how students benefit from the teacher training and of which interventions have to be done on an individual level or on the level of a general approach. The choice for a self assessment instruments shows to be the right choice. Students are capable to assess their well-being and involvement. But there is more. They seem to be the experts we need to know what to be done in teacher training to improve the curriculum. Their comments and remarks are very relevant and discreet. With this system the students will have a voice in decision making at the level of all relevant aspects of teacher training.

But also at the individual level the instrument is showing hopeful perspectives for those learners that have difficulties in making the transfer to the second year. Although we couldn't reach all students, we have some indications that the instruments empower students and enables them to deal more successfully with the problems they encounter. The result of this being: an improved quality of the training expressed in a higher level of well-being and of involvement in the students... and the lecturers.

CONCLUSIONS AND REFLECTIONS
Ferre Laevers

1 What we retain from each contribution

Michaela Ulich and Tony Mayr have brought insights at three levels. The first, much appreciated contribution, is about the concept of involvement. They added to the theoretical underpinning of this concept by linking it to a series of related terms. Most striking is their conclusion that involvement as a single concept 'is addressing motivational, emotional and cognitive aspects of a child's activity."

At the level of the use of the scale by practitioners they make very evident how cultural aspects affect the way tools are accepted and used. As to the context of the German practitioners in the area of early childhood education they conclude that on the one hand the concept of involvement "is immediately appealing to German practitioners and it fits well into the German educational culture." On the other hand, "in an early childhood culture where systematic observation and documentation is unusual" the use of the scale in everyday practice is not evident.

Finally the research reported shows some thought provoking results as to the levels of involvement linked to types of activities. The patterns observed lead to three challenging questions:

How do we have to deal with the gender-based preferences showing higher levels of involvement in girls for "more sedentary, language-related and 'school-oriented' activities", whereas boys are more engaged in "more expansive and manual/technical activities"?

How can we raise the levels of involvement in ethnic minority children, especially in language related activities where their involvement is significantly lower?

Why are younger children in the observed (all mixed-aged groups) doing poorer in terms of involvement and how can we create for them a better learning environment?

Maria Nabuco and Silvério Prates integrated the observation of involvement in a wider research project looking at the effect of in-service training. In a pre- and post-test design she focused on the 'context' and registered the improvement of quality with the ECERS-R. For a sample of three classes the Leuven Involvement Scale was used. Because of the limited sample, this research is exploratory in nature. Again challenging questions arise:

183

Why is the group with the younger children (3 years of age) showing again lower levels of involvement than the other groups of 4- and 5-year olds? Why are these lower levels linked with a better profile in terms of the ECERS-R results?

Diane Doble Leemans offers in her description of a most personal journey as a researcher and practitioner insights that support the process-oriented approach in many ways.

At the methodological level she shows how in depth research is a process of growing self-awareness that needs to be supported by a systematic inner dialogue. The author shows how the use of "work journals" can fulfil this purpose.

The approach is particularly important when observing children and trying to figure out the sense of their activities and levels of involvement. Most of the content revealed by the 'work journals' is about the self-awareness of involvement by adults and children.

A third contribution links with the adult style. This key concept in the description of the experiential approach gets a further theoretical clarification through the Manens' term 'pedagogical tact' and putting it into the perspective of the phenomenographic approach. A striking link as well is with the concept of the 'intuitive practitioner', making clear that the experiential style is based on the capacity of the adult to sense intuitively what is taking place 'on the other side'.

Finally, the focus on visual expression in children, supports three conclusions: it makes us aware that this type of activities, as witnessed by the Reggio Emilia pedagogy, are crucial in the construction of meaning, it is the privileged locus for high levels of involvement and it demands the highest level of 'pedagogical tact' from the adult in order to really support the process.

In the Effective Early Learning project (EEL) adult style is considered one of the key factors in realising quality. The research reported by Christine Pascal and Tony Bertram covers a large amount of data collected in a wide variety of settings. The overall conclusion is that practitioners tend to display a high level of sensitivity in their interaction with children. At the same time giving autonomy - involving children in decisions and the setting of rules and respecting the choices children make – seems to be the more difficult kind of interventions. Further the data prove that efforts to help teachers to develop a more child-centred approach are rewarded. For the three dimensions an improvement of the quality of the interactions was registered in nearly all types of settings.

The most thought-provoking part of the results is to be found in the comparison between the several types of settings. The following questions emerge when we look at the profiles:

184

Why are the levels for sensitivity – in the first round - the lowest in Playgroups, while one would expect that this dimension, closest to common sense pedagogy, would be the strongest asset of the voluntary sector?

In general the Nursery School and the Private Day Nursery deliver more quality than other settings when observing the interactions. Is this linked to the rich child-centred tradition of this kind of settings? Does the comparison with the reception classes confirm the general opinion that these are more influenced by a more formal approach of the primary schools?

What can we learn from the sometimes dramatic improvement of the adult style, especially in the Playgroups, about the learning processes of adults? Is there evidence that the poorer the initial training, the higher the effect of intervention?

Marjatta Kalliala and Leena Tahkokallio succeeded in combining both quality indicators in their study: they gathered systematically information about both involvement and adult style. This research has also an interesting comparative dimension as far as data from the U.K. have been included in the reflections.

A first, striking result, is that the levels of involvement rose in all day-care centres as a consequence of the support sessions with the practitioners. In the first year the impact of the sessions on style was evident: there was an increase for Sensitivity and for Stimulation, while Autonomy dropped. In the second year the pattern remained stable and reflected the levels reached at the end of the year before.

The comparison with the British data was surprising. Especially the low score for Autonomy in Britain (in the first measurement) contrasted with the high level for this dimension in the Finnish settings.

The data and reflections of the authors lead us to the following hypotheses:
- there is a link between the high status of 'autonomy' in the Finnish culture (leading to more permissiveness) and the high level of Autonomy on the observation scale.
- the ideal style is characterised by a high level of Sensitivity (placing the pivoting point in the middle) and a balance between Autonomy and Stimulation.
- learning to focus on 'involvement' has much to do with 'learning to take the perspective of the child' and as such seems to trigger off a developmental process resulting in a more effective adult style.
- while levels of involvement can alter year after year because a new cohort of children are observed, adult style is a rather stable factor: the competence reached is reappearing in the next year.

Julia Formosinho's contribution covers the two concepts – adult style and

185

involvement – separately. In a first part a qualitative analysis of teachers' thoughts about the use of the involvement scale reveals how this instrument in a self-evident way inspired them to take action. When low levels of involvement are observed, practitioners start to analyse the situation and seek ways to get more intrinsic motivated activity. Where this movement, originally targets the group as a whole, gradually also the individual child gets into focus and specific interventions become part of the teaching. Further involvement and the related concepts are operating as a kind of 'language' one can use to 'reconstruct' reality and structure ones narratives about practice. This insight certainly sheds a new and original light upon ways the concept of 'involvement' inform practice. In a second part adult style is addressed. Again a comparative dimension is brought, leading to the conclusion that, in contrast to the 'British pattern' – with low levels for Autonomy - Portuguese practitioners tend to be lowest in Stimulation. Again an attempt is made to conceptualise the pattern and link it with the cultural background. The high level of Sensitivity can be interpreted as a reflection of 'respect for the child' observable in "the tone of voice, in the gesture, in visual contact, in listening, in encouragement, in empathy for the child's needs and concerns". The rather high level of Autonomy witnesses "belief in the child's competence in the area of self-initiated activity".

From the reflections made by the author two questions arise:

Can we substantiate the link between the attitude of 'respect for the child' as an attitude and the dimension of Sensitivity in the scale? Can we do the same for 'belief in the child's competence' and high levels on the scale for 'Autonomy'.

Can we relate Vygotsky's insights about the role of the adult with the dimensions of Autonomy and Stimulation and if so, what would be the consequence of this at the level of the operationalisation of these subscales?

In their support of families living in difficult conditions, Gabriela Portugal and Paulo Santos were inspired by the experiential framework and in particular by the Adult Style instrument. Their main contribution consists in transferring the scales for the three dimensions to the level of family support workers and their interactions with families. In a convincing way they show how the concepts of Sensitivity, Autonomy and Stimulation can function as tools to understand what happens in the interaction between professionals and families. This exercise not only results in a new instrument (with a new field of application) but strengthens at the same time the conceptual basis of the Adult Style Observation Schedule. A series of narratives show the depth in the reflection of professionals when using the framework and the impact of it in an area where finding the delicate balance between types of interventions is difficult and at the same time crucial.

Peter Van Sanden and An Joly's story about the use of the process-oriented approach brings us in Nicaragua where they supported an innovative project aiming at the inclusion of handicapped children in the regular school system. Their contribution in the project and at the Socrates conference in December was enriching and therefore integrated in this report.

The work they shared was about the implementation of the experiential approach using the 'Process Oriented Child Monitoring' as tool. This is a complex instrument that starts with a screening of each of the children in the group for well-being and involvement and ends with interventions to improve the levels for the group and for individual children. The main insights brought by this meticulous reconstruction of a process taking more than a year are:

- the starting point – that is: the assessment of the overall level of well-being and involvement for each child – is a process on its own. One of the indications for the assimilation of the concepts is the competence to make the distinction between involvement and well-being.

- throughout the Action-Reflection cycles the practitioners adopt a more realistic attitude towards their assessments. They learn to see that giving high scores without good reason doesn't help them to improve their practice. This shift is most important when the instrument is leading them to the analysis of the conditions affecting the levels of well-being and involvement. Contrary to the assessment of the process-variables, here they have to unveil their own role in the emergence of well-being and involvement.

- one of the most important indications for the development of a more process-oriented attitude is the changed view on the status of play. Whereas originally, as a part of the culture of the education system in which they are embedded, play is seen as unimportant leisure time and consequently neglected, another attitude occurs. With the systematic analysis of everyday practice play is gradually seen as a rich area that deserves attention and stimulation in order to boast the levels of involvement.

Ludo Heylen's contribution gives ideas for new impulses in teacher training. By introducing a self assessment instrument based on the concepts of well-being and involvement, teacher training can be based on the same concepts as the schools where the students will be employed in the future. The self assessment instrument is apart of a system that can lead to two different tracks: one that can ensure a better individual support for students that are in danger to drop out and one that can enrich the discussion about curriculum changes. Track one gives possibilities to get special attention for those students that have problems in making the transfer to the next year. Especially students from ethnic minorities can be supported this way. Track two enables to get a better picture of which courses are reaching high level of involvement and which courses aren't. It is striking to see that in the discussions students are showing -very discreetly and loyal to the lecturers- to be the experts in what can be changed in order to make things run better. Within the different settings of the action-research it shows that this Student Monitoring System (SMS-EXE) invites students to develop disposistions like reflective thinking, self management and self regulation and participation in decision making.

2 Closing reflections

When looking at the harvest of this Socrates project one can only be impressed by the many insights that were generated through the network of partners. It is obvious that the chosen strategy – focusing on two central concepts – proved to be effective.

The overall conclusion from the reports is that the process-oriented approach and the related concepts and instruments offer a useful and inspiring framework to understand what happens in practice and take initiatives that improve the quality of the work. One of the authors witnesses that "these were high quality empowering tools for teachers and researchers". Contrary to traditional instruments only used by university professors the concepts were made accessible to the practitioners, hence the "easy acceptance of core concepts".

Another striking element is that the concepts are applicable in a very wide variety of settings and situations. Because of that they offer an ideal entrance or window for comparative research. Differences in patterns between different cultures became obvious when comparing the data for the Adult Style. In another way the application of the instruments in new contexts, such as the interaction from professional support workers and families, was an indication for the potential of the concepts.

As part of the added value of this project we can refer to the several contributions at the level of the concepts: the triangular model proposed to represent the balance between the three dimensions of style, the link with the concept of 'pedagogical tact', the reference to Vygotsky when reflecting on Autonomy. Other insights are about the process of implementation, such as the recognition that learning to observe involvement can on its own have a positive impact on the adult style.
One reflection retained our attention in a particular way: the conclusion phrased in the report of the Nicaraguan project and stating that the process-oriented approach can help practitioners to see how much they can do for the benefit of children just by giving the best of themselves – before getting at the point

where material conditions limit the possible impact of their work. This is an interesting conclusion from a project aiming at inclusive education. Showing that making efforts to get higher levels of well-being and involvement to a certain extend is at the reach of any educational system.